hear the CHILDREN laughing

TALES FROM AN AID WORKER

LIZ HOBBS

First published in Goolwa SA 2023
Publication assistance by Immortalise

ISBN – print: 978-0-6452473-1-2
ISBN – ebook: 978-0-6452473-2-9

Cover by Josefine Lea Dohm
Internal art by Liz Hobbs
Typesetting and ebook format by Ben Morton

This is a work of autobiographical fiction. Some tales have only names and/or settings changed; some have composite characters or are made up of composite events, based on my lived experience. In some, the remembered setting is the backdrop of a fictional tale.

For those who wish to understand the context of these tales, I suggest you refer to the Epilogue, where, under the country headings, I have attempted to explain the situations in which I found myself.

Finally I wish to state that in no way do I represent any company or organization mentioned within. The views expressed are solely mine and are only based on my memory of events.

Liz Hobbs

Dear God,

We pray for another way of being: another way of knowing.

Across the difficult terrain of our existence we have attempted to build a highway and in so doing have lost our footpath. God lead us to our footpath: Lead us there where in simplicity we may move at the speed of natural creatures and feel the earth's love beneath our feet. Lead us there where step-by-step we may feel the movement of creation in our hearts. And lead us there where side-by-side we may feel the embrace of the common soul. Nothing can be loved at speed.

God lead us to the slow path; to the joyous insights of the pilgrim; another way of knowing: another way of being.

Amen.

Courtesy of Michael Leunig.

CONTENTS

HOME?

Is This Home?

Pat was five minutes early. Through the window I could see her marching up Dad's garden path, the hydrangeas and azaleas a blaze of colour to either side of her.

I opened the door.

'Buff old girl! Here—a big hug!'

How quickly she masked her shock.

'Auntie Pat! What a pleasure!'

'All mine,' she countered briskly as she broke off and strode into the hall. 'The point is, I'm here, you're back in Australia, and with a jolly good story to tell, I'll bet.' There was a melting fondness in her gaze.

I ushered her into the lounge.

Vera and Dad were standing stiffly in the middle of the vast, carpeted room. Dad had his doctor look, dressed in his charcoal suit, and Vera's salmon pink silk said everything.

'Good evening. Good evening!' Pat said cheerily as she gave my dad and his new wife a firm handshake. 'And how are you both?'

'We're very well thank you,' Vera said pleasantly. 'Do sit down, Pat.' She indicated a red velvet chair.

'Can we get you a sherry?' said Dad.

'Don't mind if I do. I'm parched.' Pat plonked herself in the chair.

Dad turned to me, 'Offer your aunt the hors d'oeuvres, Buff.' It was an order. I felt myself stiffen.

Pat turned to me, patting the chair next to her. 'Sit ye down and tuck into something yourself. Some fattening up wouldn't do you any harm,' she said firmly. 'Now, I want to hear all about it.'

I sat down next to my aunt. 'Where to start?' I said tentatively. I'd hardly spoken about this since I'd come home.

'Wherever you want to, dear. You were working in the most poverty-stricken country in the world. Were you sick?'

'Well I guess so, but everyone was sick or dying. It seemed the norm.'

My voice sounded different, like I was talking from the bottom of the sea.

'Hard for us to fathom here,' Pat said loudly, throwing a look at her sister-in-law.

'Yes. The mortality age is forty-five. The lottery is more about what kills you, not when.'

Pat paused. 'And you?'

'When we reached the tropical medicine clinic in London they found we had all sorts of exotic parasites. My co-worker had hookworm, amoebic dysentery ... '

Pat was quiet for a bit, slowly nodding her head. She turned to Vera who was now adrift in the middle of the room. 'Come and sit down, Vera. Can't be standing around all day.' She smiled at her new sister-in-law. 'You must be so proud of this stepdaughter of yours,' she said, giving me a gentle pat on my knee.

'We certainly are,' Vera said cautiously.

I was becoming acutely aware of my op-shop clothing and torn sandals. This other world of Adelaide was so far away from my present inner reality. Now Dad was making his way across the room with a silver tray bearing crystal glasses of sherry. 'We're looking forward to seeing the slides, aren't we dear?' he said to Vera.

Pat turned to me again. 'Here, stuff your face with some of this, love,' she said, passing the plate, 'Put a bit of fat on!'

I gave her a little grin. 'Yes, there wasn't much food. We tried to keep the lurgies out of our drinking water with iodine—my teeth went purple.' I bared my teeth, caught Dad's eye and looked down. This wasn't going well.

'Well now, there's a new look!' Pat guffawed.

I glanced over at Vera. Dad was sitting so close to her on the couch that they seemed to be glued together at the knee.

Pat raised her glass to them. 'Bottoms up,' she said.

'Cheers,' they murmured.

Pat turned to me again. 'So, are we going to do this slide-show or not?'

'Yes, get a wriggle on, Buff,' Dad said brusquely. 'We don't want the roast to burn, do we?' He laughed.

I squirmed in the small silence. 'I just wanted you guys to know what I've been doing,' I said quietly.

'Speak up, I can't hear you,' shouted Dad from the couch.

'Ready to roll!' I shouted back. 'Lights off!'

Pat winked at me.

'This is a photo of the food convoy.' I was deliberately keeping my voice matter-of-fact. 'You can see they're old trucks—there were thirty —and it took five nights to travel from Kassala in Sudan, through Eritrea and into Tigray in Ethiopia—actually it took a whole month to get there from Adelaide. On the convoy we could only travel at night because of the bombers.' I stopped.

Dad was plumping up a cushion behind his wife. 'We'll have to get our maps out, won't we,' he joked.

I caught Pat's eye and turned away. 'There were only three expatriates on the convoy. We were put into separate trucks—two missionary priests in one and me in the other. We slept in caves or in the forest during the days, but it was terribly, terribly hot. I couldn't sleep in all that time.'

Pat's voice was gentle. 'You felt too unsafe to sleep, Buff?'

I could feel myself choking up. Choking up was the last thing I needed right now. I took a deep breath. 'It was funny in the first cave— there were only two beds made of stone. Four fighters usually slept on them, two to a bed, but they kindly gave them up for us. It meant that the priests had either to sleep with me or with each other. They slept spooned together, snoring their heads off and dressed in dark grey suits!' I laughed, and I knew it sounded too loud.

Pat grinned. 'You could have made it a threesome and then four of the fighters could have had a bed.' I could see she was needling Dad. Long history there.

I changed the slide. A burnt-out truck was lying on its side. 'This is how it is. Lots of the trucks get bombed bringing food in. We weren't, thank God, but we did have one MIG fly really low over us when we were hidden in the forest. The convoy is the lifeline for five million people. Almost their only source of food.'

I glanced over at Dad. His spine seemed to be almost shooting sparks. My fury went up a notch. I could feel my voice cracking. 'They are the bravest, most beautiful people I have met in my entire life. You've got no idea how hard it is for them! How hard it is even to bring food in—the armed guards sitting on the cabin roof night after night, convoy after convoy, the land mines, the snipers, the bombers and no rain, no water, no food … ' I could hear myself. I was a mess. Any minute I'd start crying. Oh hell!

'Go on, Buff, sweetie,' said Pat gently. Now she glanced over at Dad. He and Vera were sitting like twin statues now.

I wanted to run. I changed the slide. 'Well anyway, the convoy got lost in the Eritrean desert. We'd camped in a forest next to a bombed-out airfield and then set off at night, but I was in one of six trucks that got lost. We were going round and round on the sand with a whole night full of stars above us and dawn was coming and there weren't any trees to camouflage the trucks from the bombers when it got light. I pointed out the Southern Cross to the driver and we followed that, then the truck in front tipped over and we were in a ravine and we were stuck —couldn't go back, couldn't go forward … '

Words were tumbling out of my mouth.

'Next slide. Oh, that's one of the nomads. He was the tallest, gentlest man. They came over the hill with some camels and goats just as the sun came up, and as soon as they saw our predicament they started gathering up the food from the tipped truck, carrying it sack by sack on their shoulders, up the hill, away from bombers. They saved every drop of that food—all of them working together. It took hours … '

'And you, Buff?' It was Dad, his voice gruff.

Pat shot a look at her brother.

'That old guy brought me milk,' I went on. 'And they watched me drink it. They didn't have any food themselves … so … the next slide,'

Dad suddenly stood up. 'Just a minute!' he shouted.

I jolted back and stared at him. Standing there, he quickly collected himself, almost like he was spooning himself back into his suit. It was a mannerism I recognized. 'Vera has to check the roast,' he said smoothly, as if nothing had happened. 'We can't have it spoil, can we?' He turned to Pat. 'Another sherry while she crisps up the potatoes?'

'No,' said Pat very firmly, standing up to come and sit next to me 'What a terrifying story, Buff.'

Tears welled again. My words had dried up.

Pat gently put her hand over mine. 'You must have felt so alone.'

Still I couldn't say anything. My thoughts were out of control. There hadn't been enough water to drink; I'd been so frightened that I couldn't make spit in my mouth; I'd thought the tipped truck had been land-mined; I'd been certain they were coming to shoot us.

'Well if you don't want a drink, I think I'll pour myself one,' said Dad loudly. 'Could we have the light on, Buff?'

I stood up and went to turn it on.

After a while Vera returned from the kitchen and I could see her taking in the scene. 'It'll be ready in fifteen minutes,' she said quickly. 'Nothing like good old roast lamb.'

'Okay. Shall I move on?' I asked.

'Abso-bloody-lutely,' said Pat firmly. The light was turned off again.

'This is the military hospital where I stayed for five months. As you can see, it's in the mountains—lots of monkeys and apes.'

'I can't see anything, Buff,' said Dad.

Rage was at boiling point. 'No. I often put this slide in when I'm giving lectures,' I said pointedly as I stood up and went to the screen with a ruler. 'See this hill—that's the X-ray department. See the valley—there are 20 wards down there. And see this cliff? That's where they did surgery at night. All camouflaged. The farmers are ploughing all around with their oxen to make it look like farmland.'

I paused. No one spoke. 'They had five doctors for five million people. So the surgeons were actually health-workers trained in only four months—doing amputations, all sorts.' At last I could feel real strength come back into my voice. 'But you know, even there, when they were supposed to all be equal, the 'surgeons' wore red berets. You can't get away from hierarchy can you?' I shot a look at Dad. It wasn't nice.

'This is a hospital ward. They lie in the dark, side by side on a long stone bed.

'Next slide. This is us. We're giving a lesson under the tree so the bombers don't see us. See the skeleton we made from cardboard? All our students are young people who were injured in the war.'

'So, Buff, where did you sleep?' Dad was leaning forward now. The sherry in his hand was trembling.

I barely noticed. 'In a cave. We had stone beds and our share of spiders and scorpions and rats. You should have seen our armed guard, Pat,' I said, continuing to ignore Dad. 'His name was Beyene and his job was to protect us from the hyenas. They'd got used to eating dead bodies on the battlefields and were dangerous. I guess Beyene was also protecting us from snipers. I think he was gay—the sweetest man. We used to be scared of going to the loo at night, and it wasn't just because of the hyenas, the loo was sitting on the edge of a cliff—a drop toilet with a platform with lots of holes. We all thought it was like Russian Roulette—who was going to fall in first.' I laughed.

Dad now said quietly, almost a whisper, 'Buff it wasn't even your war. You might have died.' Was that voice choked? Or a reprimand? I didn't know.

Pat turned to me. 'Actually it was Mengistu, wasn't it? The dictator who the Tigrayans overthrew? The Israelis and the Russians supplied the weapons to prop up that disgusting regime. More deaths than El Alamein in just one of the battles.'

'Yes. I was teaching some basic physiotherapy to prevent disability following injuries. Our students followed the war front all the way to Addis Ababa and ... '

I looked around at Dad, shocked to see something that looked like unshed male tears. Could that be right?

'That's it,' I said.

There was silence in the room. I stood up abruptly. 'Roast time, I think. Thanks everyone for listening. I'd better help with the dinner.' I stood up, turned on the light and walked out of the room.

In the passage I could hear them talking. Dad's voice sounded all funny. 'I've no idea where she gets it from. I've told her it's not her war, not her country. We had to go to war. We had to defend the Empire. She doesn't.' He sounded confused.

'Maybe it's time we all moved on from the ways of the British Empire, don't you think?' said Pat.

'I don't know. I'm getting too old for this.' There was silence for a bit before he added, 'I don't understand or even believe in what she's been doing, Pat, but I'm damned proud of her.'

Did I hear it right? Could I possibly have heard it right?

I made my way down to the kitchen.

An hour later I found myself alone with Pat as I escorted her to her car.

'I've got a funny sense that the project didn't work out too well for you in Tigray, Buff,' she said quietly. 'Am I right?'

I faltered. A car roared up the street, its headlights blazing. Gradually the noise died down until all I could hear was an automatic sprinkler softening the silence. At last I turned to Pat. 'It was the hardest thing I've ever done.' The gentle sound of a Chopin nocturne floated from a nearby house. 'One of our students was a planted spy for the Derg; they'd run out of plaster of Paris for all the fractures; the disabled were stigmatized; the interpreters were in a power struggle … ' I stopped. Tears were welling up again. 'And even with all that … I should have … even trying as hard as I possibly could … I still couldn't … '

Pat glanced back at the house before enfolding me in a hug. Her voice was firm when she said, 'It depends how you define 'good enough', love. Difficult things are just what they are: difficult.' I let myself melt into the strength of her. 'You've always been good enough, Buff, even without battling the war zones.'

We stood there, the nocturne soft in the background.

Finally I broke the silence. 'I'd still prefer it if you didn't tell Dad.'

'Of course not. I wasn't born yesterday.' Pat climbed into her old car. She wound down her window. 'Your dad does care, you know. He's a silly old coot. Just got it all bottled up in there with a big cork keeping it down. The Middle East almost did that brother of mine in: we called it shell shock back then. Now it's called post-traumatic stress, but there's no way he'd ever let on.'

Comprehension flooded through me as I watched her car bunny hopping down the road.

MEXICO

WHAT HAS HAPPENED TO AJOYA?

I'm picking my way through samphire on a clay pan. It's early morning in the South Australian desert. The dogs bound ahead after a rabbit, barking happily as they chase in and out of the coolabah trees.

Suddenly I turn. There on the horizon is the sun. It's a Mexican sun. Huge and blazing red. And immediately I find myself back beside the wide riverbed in Ajoya. I can even hear the donkeys braying and the clucking of chickens as that big red sun rises up.

Memories flood in.

I see the river snaking through the valley below the village, and a woman in a wide hat riding a horse side-saddle, the horse's hooves clattering on the pebbles. I see that sun pounding down, throwing sharp shadows on the mud huts and the sandy streets; columns of smoke spiralling up from the village and melding with the smell of damp earth, pigs and the horse's flanks.

And so many special people:

Jose Maria driving a taxi without a windscreen and using his crutches instead of feet on the pedals; Pablo with the gunshot leg; young Manolito and his watermelon smile as he learned to point to pictures. And Bepe, who'd had a wall collapse on him, laboriously painting Manolito's new wooden chair; Consuela, in her wheelchair, proudly nursing her newborn baby; Juan, so passionately in love with Maria.

I remember the soft evenings under the spreading tree, singing to guitars and listening to the sound of children laughing.

I also remember the fear. Gun shots in the night; drunken brawls and whisperings about the drug barons; the forbidden crops defended by machine guns. And Pablo's daughter and her husband sneaking across the border into USA; the fear in their kitchen as Carmela prepared food for their journey over the mountains.

And now? Silence.

Two Australians murdered. Kidnappings. Violence. Drug cartels swallowing up this little village, these mountains. I can't blame the farmers for growing opium instead of corn. But at what cost? At what terrible cost?

Here, now, in safety, I sit down in the quiet. The sun is up and the Australian desert horizon stretches in a vast arc. A lonely crow squarks from a dead tree. The dogs trot back to me, tongues hanging, tails wagging.

Time to boil the billy for a cup of tea.

CONEJA

I sit in the back of an old green truck, grinding over the cobbles in the Mexican *pueblo*. Deep purple mountains stretch away behind the mud huts, and spirals of blue smoke rise up from little fires in the predawn mountain light. Beside me are the men I know from the Project PROJIMO.

'*Hombre!*' shouts Pedro above the din of the truck. '*Tengo hambre!*' His mates nod amiably as Pedro peeks into his little cloth bundle of *tortillas*. Warm steam escapes, steeped in the homely aroma of corn. 'Not yet, *amores*,' he croons to the food.

His friends laugh. They understand: it's all very well to be hungry but it'll be six hours to Mazatlan, even if the truck doesn't die on the road from sheer exhaustion. It'd be crazy to eat the one meal now.

Next to me, Manolo hefts himself onto a sack behind the cabin of the truck, stacking his crutches beside him. '*Dios*, can this old fart belch out smoke!' he shouts. 'If our lungs don't collapse from diesel, our balls'll drop off with cold!' He laughs loudly, and shows a set of tiny teeth, an apology in that strong chiselled face.

Everyone agrees that they're hungry, but they shrug as they pull grey rugs over their heads and around themselves. 'Murdering bastard, the cold.'

They nod to me, well wrapped in my blanket.

Manolo leans back on the cabin and closes his eyes. Lost in thought, Pedro scratches his crotch while the others shift from one sack to another, trying to get comfortable. Eyes close as we settle in for the long haul.

But no! The truck grinds to a halt; eyes blink open. We're outside the Project at the end of the long street. Now what? A woman in black shrills at the truck driver, a bunch of scrawny kids beside her. Cadging a ride? All eight of them?

'Damn. The sardine treatment again,' mutters Pedro.

As the woman haggles, we shiver until finally Manolo bangs his fist on the cabin roof. 'This'd freeze the tits off your mother, Juan!' he yells. 'Move it!'

But the woman is in no hurry. She continues to barter until satisfied. Then without further ado she turns to one of the children sitting on the road, lifts him up and plonks him on the tray of the truck. His thin legs land awkwardly, like a new-born colt.

Now she dumps a red cloth bundle over the side beside the boy, saying as it lands, '*Hasta luego*, Paolito,' her tone matter-of-fact.

The truck starts up; finally we're moving. The woman doesn't wave and neither does the boy as she turns and walks back up the road with her brood of little ones. Soon out of sight, gears grinding, the truck starts on the mountain descent.

We turn to appraise the newcomer, the men's gaze frank.

He's a thin child, perhaps ten years old, looking ready to burst with excitement and fear, judging by that watermelon smile and the wide eyes. Two huge front teeth protrude between his lips. A *morena* for sure. I love these Mexican Indians. Such special people. This boy can't be anything else with his slanted eyes, high cheekbones and brown skin.

17

Much like the men really, though sadly they'd never admit it. Is this the first time the kid has been outside his *pueblo*?

Relaxing on their sacks, the men watch as the boy struggles for that 'matter-of-factness' his mother had displayed so easily. He hauls his little body onto a box, gathering his meagre cloth bundle close. Now we can see that one leg is paralysed, probably from polio. Not so different from Manolo, whose plastic splint is half hidden inside his boot.

Manolo leans over to the boy, his eyes kindly.

'*Ola, coneja!*'

The boy looks up, startled. Rabbit?

'Australia—that's the place for you—lots of rabbits there. You could go and join Liz here. She lives with all those rabbits.'

We laugh and the boy's gaze scuttles from one face to another.

'*Y mia Mama?*' he asks in a small voice, trying to hide his teeth with his lips.

The man leans over and tickles him roughly on the chest. Some of his fingers are crooked. '*Y tua Mama? Porque tua Mama?* Come and sit over here with me.'

Tentatively the boy hitches himself a little closer and sits on another sack.

'Little rabbit, do you know what these are?' Manolo asks as he points to the lengths of wood beside him.

'No.'

'They're crutches and I made them.'

'Why?' asks the boy.

'So I can do whatever I want to do,' replies Manolo. 'And now I want to sit in the back of a truck with a rabbit and watch the world go by.'

He tickles the boy again. '*Basta! Basta!*' the boy shrieks.

Manolo stops and looks at him, his eyes suddenly gentle.

'And what do you want to do, little rabbit?' he asks.

The boy looks up with shining eyes. 'I want to go to Mazatlan,' he says firmly.

'Do you go to school?'

'No,' he replies with a slight lift of his chin. He turns to watch the countryside moving slowly past. Pepe looks at Manolo and raises an eyebrow.

'Why don't you go to school?' presses Manolo.

'It's too far from home.' His gaze wanders now from the donkeys by the side of the road, to an old man in black sitting near some cactus on the hill.

'But can't your Mama take you?'

'No,' says the boy, turning his head as a yellow bus with men sitting on the roof speeds past them. 'I don't have a wheelchair,' he adds as an afterthought.

Manolo frowns, looking down on the little tousled head, and on to the distant hills behind.

'Well, let's go to Mazatlan then,' he says quietly.

The boy looks up at him, his innocence as clear as the sky. 'Well that's where I'm going! I don't know about you,' he pipes, his face all smiles.

He's soon chattering like a little monkey, pointing out to Manolo a wayside shrine covered in flowers, a herd of goats, a mountain crag. It seems this child has never seen so much in one day. He looks quickly from one thing to another in order to see as much as possible. Jiggling with excitement he takes in the cobbled streets, policemen in strange uniforms, crowds of women dressed in black filing into a house, and trucks and trucks and trucks full of people.

Our truck rumbles into the main square of a larger town and stops. As the driver gets out to stretch, Pedro springs over the side and sprints across to a red and white striped awning. Soon he returns, holding a huge green ice cream, shaped like a Christmas tree. With an easy smile he hands it to the boy.

'Gracias,' his little mouth mumbles through teeth as he stares at the ice cream in amazement. 'Where did you get all that money?' he asks.

Embarrassed, Pedro shrugs and lifts himself aboard again, his plastic sandals thumping onto the tray. He pulls out his bundle of *tortillas*, now no longer steaming, and begins to eat.

Manolo catches Pedro's eye and grins. He pretends not to watch the boy hesitate before the latter tears the ice cream down the middle. With grubby hands, dripping milk all over the truck tray, he hands half to Manolo, who takes it without a fuss. He eats his share with his arm around the boy, an easy gesture.

We're going faster now that we've reached the bitumen. Our hair streaks behind us and our eyelashes turn inside out, making us squint.

Shivering, the boy snuggles close to Manolo.

'What will you do in Mazatlan?' the latter shouts.

'Sit on the street. Mama says people will just give money to me. Uncle will carry me there.' He looks up, his eyes shining with pride.

Manolo looks out at the tomato fields, silent.

The truck slows in dense traffic, nearing the outskirts of the city. At last Manolo turns to the boy and asks, 'Coneja, you know the Project

PROJIMO in Ajoya, don't you?'

The boy doesn't answer. His gaze darts from one side of the street to the other. We can see that this city must be huge to him. Has he ever seen so many people in all his life? The kid stares at wayside stalls, garages, bars, and shops.

Manolo repeats his question carefully and more loudly, his attention riveted on the boy.

'Have you heard of the Project PROJIMO to help people with disabilities? You were standing outside it when your Mama put you on the truck. We all thought you had come from there.'

The boy looks up at last, his eyes focusing on Manolo's face.

'No,' he replies. 'Mama just brought me to catch the truck.'

'Well PROJIMO is a place for children with legs like yours. We make them braces. Braces are things that hold your legs straight so you can walk.' As he speaks he lifts his trouser leg to show the boy his own splint. 'We make wheelchairs too. We make sure kids get to school. And the Project's got a wonderful playground where all the kids play together.'

The boy's head spins around at the sight of McDonalds'.

'Oh?'

'Listen to me!' the man commands.

The boy jumps. 'Sounds nice,' he says politely.

'Yes it is nice, Coneja—much nicer than earning money on the street.'

'But Mama said ...'

'Mama doesn't know! Believe me. Look. I'm going to give you my name and telephone number.'

He tears off a piece of paper from a little notebook and scribbles on it, holding it out to the boy. 'Put it in your pocket and don't lose it—ever! Do you hear? Here's some money for the phone call. I have to get off now—but call me. Don't spend that money on anything—anything else.'

The truck pulls over in a byway next to some flat-roofed houses with iron grills over the windows. The man's hand lingers on the boy's black curls before he clambers down, crutches in hand. The truck starts up again with a roar and lumbers off, its horn blaring.

The man waves. 'I'll wait for your call, Coneja!' he yells.

The boy waves briefly, staring for a moment at the diminishing figure until the truck turns the corner. He gasps.

The sea.

His mouth falls open.

'Mazatlan, here we come!' he yells.

CARMEN

A Carmen?

Yes.

Fire smouldering in the body, dare devil black eyes, a tilt of head on a slender neck. And of course, as she should be, dressed in scarlet—a slinky scarlet dress.

She sits at the end of the project garden looking down at the village below and the wide brown river that snakes between mountains. The other girls ignore her. At the southern end of the garden they huddle their wheelchairs into a tight circle, sitting provocatively with hair sprayed and bright skirts flashing in the sun.

Their heads turn as a young man makes his way past them and down the garden path in the direction of the girl. They watch.

'*Ola*, Concita!'

She looks up, colours a little, and with a small lift of the chin, looks away.

It's the new guy. A cut above the others, and more confident. Don Jose? He swings towards her on his crutches, past the drinking fountain and exercise plinth.

'*Que tal?*'

Standing beside her, he hooks his stump on the handle of the crutch and leans nonchalantly against the tree trunk; pulls out a packet of cigarettes.

23

'Smoke?'

She takes a cigarette and places it between sensuous, red lips. As he lights it she holds his gaze with a challenging one of her own. She inhales. Exhales. Smoke curls around the stubble on his tanned cheeks.

'So?' he drawls, leaning back again on the tree.

She refuses to look up at him. 'So? So what. The city.' Her voice is husky, the tone, careless.

He lifts an eyebrow. 'Mazatlan? Might see you around.' He's matching his tone to hers.

She shrugs. 'Maybe. And maybe not.'

There's a hint of a smile on his face. 'Going to a welding job perhaps?'

'Perhaps.'

Her nonchalance is exquisite. 'Well if that's the case you could call your shop, 'No-Slope Wheelchairs.' He looks up into the tree as he says it.

'And why?' Still she refuses to look at him.

'Don't know that I'd trust the brakes you make.' He exhales a perfect ring of smoke.

'And if I take the chair that I made down the gully road to prove it?' In spite of herself, her face has reddened.

He laughs.

She flicks ash into the garden. Down below a man in a black hat leads a donkey laden with firewood along a lane. She sees the donkey pull back on the rope, splay its legs and piss into red dust. Jose notices her slight grin. She turns to him now and murmurs, 'One of the wheels wobbles on your chair. I wouldn't be seen dead in it.'

Jose, sensing his advantage, quickly drops onto the bench beside her chair. 'You were brave to join the wheelchair-building workshop—the only girl. Do you like it here?' he asks, his tone gentle now. 'Must be different living in mountains after Mazatlan.'

A soft black tendril of hair brushes Concita's shoulder in the breeze. For a brief moment, her face looks vulnerable, even child-like. 'It's okay,' she replies. She takes another quick drag on her cigarette and looks at him square. 'I like the open air.'

He catches the look deftly, says nothing. Behind them, high-pitched girly laughter pierces the soft afternoon. There is the sound of boots scuffing on sand as little Pepito struggles up and down the parallel bars in his new braces.

Jose follows her gaze. 'The open air ... ' he finally murmurs. 'Yeah. I like mountain air too.' He pauses. 'It must be a change for you, though, after Mazatlan.'

Concita stills. 'What do you mean?' She slowly pinches the end of her cigarette.

Jose takes a while to answer. 'The other guys told me your story. Your mother kept you hidden in the house for four years, right?'

Immediately he regrets it. She whips around like a toreador, eyes flashing. 'Damn you! Leave me alone!'

'Hey! Hang on a minute!'

'Damn them!' she yells as she grabs at a wheel of her chair. 'They've no right to go blabbing!' She starts to turn. 'And neither have you!'

Jose leaps up on one leg and grabs the chair to prevent her. 'Hey! Hold on!'

'Get lost!' She's clawing at his hand on the wheel. It's panic now.

Off balance, he grabs her arm to stop falling, face red. '*Madre di Dios!*' he sighs as he steadies himself and carefully sits back down, obviously shaken.

With arms wrapped around herself, she rocks back and forth; senses the hush behind her in the garden; feels all eyes trained on her back. 'I'm sorry,' she says at last, in a small voice.

Jose glowers, reaches out for his crutches and leans them next to him on the bench. He makes a show of taking out another cigarette, saying nothing.

Concita brushes her tears away irritably. 'Just don't give me any of that pity, that *menos validos* talk, okay?'

Jose shrugs. 'For God's sake! My story isn't much grander.'

The girl continues to rock. Tears of hurt pride keep welling. 'No pity, okay?' she says again.

'Well don't you give me any either. What makes you so special, eh?' he retorts. His look burns.

She shifts her weight awkwardly and stares down at the village, her eyes spilling tears. Smoke from fires spirals up into the blue. There is an everyday-ness about the sounds—of dogs, roosters and the wild cries of children.

Jose looks at her. He reaches out to gently place a hand on her knee. 'It was just a friendly enquiry,' he says. 'Only making friends. You're great—by far the most beautiful girl here.'

Concita flinches, picks up his hand from her knee and places it deliberately back on his own knee, saying nothing.

There's a slight gleam in his eye as he persists. 'So … you've enjoyed it?'

'It's been okay.' She fidgets with a little fan on her lap, one that she bought in the market. Sparks of sunlight catch her red dress.

'And?'

'I don't give a stuff!' She flashes him a dark look. 'I'll do what I damned-well like! I'll weld. If I want to. Talk with a guy. If I want to. No-one's going to push me around.'

'I've noticed that,' he drawls.

Far below, dogs are fighting and children laugh as they play on the river's edge. She takes a while to speak. 'To hell with the tumour,' she says, her voice so low he has to lean forward to hear her. 'To hell with God's punishment.'

Jose caresses a red hibiscus in his hands, plucked from the nearby bush. 'God's punishment, they said? Yeah, yeah. I know that one. Some God, huh?' He flicks a look at her cleavage as he says this.

She doesn't see the look. 'Puts you off believing in God,' she replies, throwing her half-cigarette over the cliff.

His voice is silky: 'You could believe in me.' He leans forward and slips the hibiscus into her cleavage with a warm grin.

Concita crushes the flower and hurls it into the bushes. 'Damn you men and damn God too!' she yells. Long hair flying, she spins the chair and speeds away towards the women's quarters.

Jose watches her retreating form, her golden skin gleaming intermittently in the shade. He sees the other girls' smirking faces as she speeds past them.

He watches as she reaches the door, stops and turns. Her head tilts a little. She locks her gaze to his and …

Was it a smile?

Projimo

I'm crying. I feel stupid for crying. No! It's more than that. I'm aghast at myself for crying. So I'm hiding like a limp coward in the corner of the project yard, hoping no one sees me. I'd be so ashamed.

I can see Maria, wheeling her way down the path to the washing trough, the baby on her lap. The children are squealing in the playground. There's a screech of metal in the wheelchair-making workshop, and Alejandro, the old guy with the head injury is wandering around with a paintbrush in his hand. And here I am in the corner, pieces of wood and saws and glue all around me, and I'm weeping like a child.

I feel so small. For goodness sake, I could have said no!

I fish in my pocket for a damp piece of loo paper and wipe my drippy nose. I almost never cry. But, if I'm brutally honest, I sometimes cry because I'm angry.

Am I angry? I've no right to be angry. Of course not! I'm excited by the way these people have taken charge.

But ... I've come all the way from Australia to Mexico. I've got something to offer. I'm sure I could make a difference.

And no one's taken a scrap of notice. They haven't asked one single question. They haven't even noticed that I'm *not* around!

Well okay. Of course it's David they adore. I see that. He did all this. When he walks into the little clinic room in the mornings, faces light up. So different from a clinic room in Australia where professionals make sure they keep their status—I don't think they even realize there that they're doing it.

Here, it's a whole different way of being together. I love the equality. Here, the kids chat confidently with David as he squats down to their level. They all have so much fun and everyone's included. He makes mistakes and owns them. He also likes to pull up his jeans to show the kids his own splint; show them he's just like them. An amazing human being—kind, fun, and innovative.

And right now, he's giving me the absolute shits. How dare he make me feel 'less than'.

Why didn't I bring more tissues?

It happened this morning. I'd been ignored as usual, and then, right in the middle of today's clinic, a woman walked in with a sweet little girl with big black eyes who had cerebral palsy. David was examining her, making her laugh, and suddenly he turned to me and, in front of the crowd, told me to go outside and make the child a wooden seat. He must have had a pretty good idea that I don't have carpentry skills. I'm a physiotherapist. So why didn't he ask me about exercises, or positioning? No. I had to make a chair. They didn't even tell me where I could find the wood, or a hammer, or nails, or wood glue.

My gut feeling tells me it was deliberate. Or am I being paranoid? I do have jet lag and culture shock. Or is it, as my gut tells me, 'saw my legs off and cut out my tongue'?

Feeling more humiliated every minute, I was told that if I could get myself a ladder, I could probably find a few spare nails and some other bits and pieces in the workshop ceiling, and some wood in the corner of the yard. Great. So half an hour later I had a hammer and ten nails and some wood and a saw. But how to make a chair?

I've no idea. It's been two hours and it's getting dark.

There's a guy here recovering from a stroke who's been building chairs for the disabled kids. I've never seen him crying.

Yes. I'm angry. I think this is their way of making it quite clear who's in power: the chair-making; the placing of expatriates with Mexican families on different streets so we can't speak English with each other; the exclusion of our input into meetings. It's all done to make sure they stay in charge. And Westerners do not.

A trial by fire. And I get it. I really do.

I give my nose another loud blow. The loo paper is sodden.

So why am I crying? Because I feel inept, irrelevant, worth nothing. And angry!

It's disempowerment.

I stare at the pieces of wood and a thought comes to me. Because I come from a place of privilege, maybe I am the thing that isn't fair?

I've now been three hours trying to build this damned chair and I give up. David finds me. I'm snotty-nosed and hidden behind the tree. He seems surprised.

'Why didn't you come and ask for help?' he asks, looking down at my blotchy face.

I shrug, and point to the apology for a chair. 'I haven't a clue about carpentry,' I say. Then I lift my chin and meet his eye. 'And my Spanish is pretty hopeless too. But I am here because I want to learn. And that's what I'm going to do.'

He hands me his handkerchief and helps me up. 'Come on. You look like you need some dinner.'

Looking back, I am eternally grateful for that chair. During the many years that followed, David was kind and generous as he shared all that was being done in this incredible project for disabled village children in the mountains, as well as in Mazatlan and Culiacan. And later, across the world. I was able to see how people found their dignity, courage and belief in themselves.

My gratitude is immense.

I needed to feel small. I needed to have every bit of advantage taken away from me so that I could experience—even for three hours—the abject feeling of disempowerment. Disempowerment—what these people experienced daily before they came to the project.

I've been humbled by all that those beautiful, brave friends taught me over the years. We've shared our hearts and our laughter. They even taught me how to build a chair.

And I, with a much greater understanding of the meaning of rehabilitation, shared my physiotherapy knowledge with them.

UNA GRANDE TORTILLA

I love Pablo. He's the first to tell you that he's ugly because of his slanting eyes. He says they're shifty. That's unfair: the slant is probably due to his Mexican-Indian genes. He is, however, sometimes pretty nifty at avoiding hard work.

Pablo's yard is hard-packed dirt that his wife sweeps each day; a place where dogs, chooks, cats and pigs roam, fornicate, scratch, relieve themselves, squeal, bark and cluck. It's like all the other yards in the Mexican *pueblo*. Yet Pablo's yard is different. In it there are nine sweet-smelling rose bushes. They're huge and lush and smothered in red or pink blooms; so loved and watered and composted and manured that they're living proof of Pablo's loving heart. Each bush is encircled with a deep trench, which he fills with a gurgle of water every afternoon before lowering his obese body onto a little wooden chair under the largest bush. There, he sniffs the fragrance and contemplates his life—a life filled with an enthusiastic indulgence in minor vices.

Pablo loves to play cards, which his wife says is a sin for women in the *pueblo* of Ajoya. Despite the sinfulness, he and I often play cards together. I teach him snap and gin rummy; he teaches me a game with a pack of cards that look like Tarot. His wife tolerates this with her usual equanimity—foreigners are a weird lot. She just smiles and keeps on sweeping or folding or yelling at a child as we while away the time at the table.

The down side of being a guest at Pablo's is having to share a double bed with his grandmother. Like an ancient prune she's always in black—even her nightdress is black. She sleeps flat on her back, her toothless mouth gaping as though she's already dead, but every hour or so, her bones shuffling and creaking, she extricates herself from the bedclothes, gropes for the chamber pot and pisses with a tinkle. Accuracy is not her forte and the odour of urine, rotten breath and lavender water seeps into the blankets and the crumbling mud walls. During the day, none of the family takes any notice of her, which begs the question: maybe she isn't actually alive at all. She never seems to eat anything.

But Pablo ... well you notice him. Pablo wants to learn.

At six o'clock every morning you see his shadow in the yard, arms folded to ward off the night-chilled mountain wind. Ignoring the stench, he talks to the sweet, milk-smelling puppy: 'ps ... pssss ... ps ... pssss ...'

And the rooster: 'Oohh ... ooohh ... ooohh.'

And to the pigs as he fills their clanking tin bowls with yellow corn: 'Wooosch ... woooshchch ... wooooooshch ... What a nice roast pork you are going to be! Oooo ... *estas carina* ...'

Every now and then he launches a swift kick at a small rump. 'You son of a bitch!' There's squealing, a cacophony of rooster alarm and all the dogs in the *pueblo* howl in harmony.

But in a flash, they're back, jostling for position at his feet—the puppy, the rooster and the pigs. 'Oh, you little beauties,' he croons as he settles in his chair under the rose tree, the big red sun peeping at the horizon. It seems he needs to think at 6 am.

After sunrise, he moves with his wife to the lean-to with the cardboard roof. Fresh maize soaks in icy lime-water, his wife's frozen, blanched hands stirring it, round and around. With a small, cheery blaze in the stone oven nearby, Pablo grinds corn with a little metal hand grinder. The smoke mingles with the sweetness of corn as it curls around the bamboo wall, condensing in the biting cold. The couple says little to each other but they smile every so often.

It seems that Pablo acknowledges his wife as the matriarch, although they both pretend otherwise. He watches as she pounds and kneads the dough, adept hands brisk on the grey stone slab. For forty years she's been doing this.

One morning Pablo breaks with the usual routine. He chuckles to himself. His thinking is bearing a little fruit.

'I have something to say,' he declares as he warms himself by the fire, his crimson shirt glowing. He clears his throat as he watches his wife working, waiting until she looks up.

'*La vida es una grande tortilla!*' he exclaims, centre-stage at last. He turns to me. 'Life is a big *tortilla!*'

His wife nods, turns back to her task, smooths out the dough with a flat stone and presses it. With an effortless flick of her wrist she flaps it down on the hot iron.

The smell of fresh-baked *tortilla* gathers five small children and the puppy into the outhouse, the children's bare toes curling on the icy dirt floor. They watch with secure expectation as dawn sunlight slants stripes across their yellow and turquoise rags. A cold wind whips around them.

The woman turns the *tortilla* and pats it quickly until it fills and expands with the hot air. She picks it up with her fingers and drops it, steaming, upside down into the waiting cloth. When there are many added to the pile, she wraps them in the cloth and carries them, still hot, to the wooden table. Pablo and the children follow close behind her black-clad figure.

At the head of the table, Pablo is content. He has borrowed a book. Entitled *Quanto*, it's an encyclopedia with pictures. With a mouth full of *tortilla* he excitedly chatters about Pablo Darwin and the theory of evolution.

'It's in the book,' he proclaims, opening it on the table.

The children play. They're not listening. The grandmother stares at her plate.

'They say our ancestors are monkeys! What a thing to say in a book. That is *tonto*! Crazy! If a dog has a baby it's a dog. Always. If a pig has a baby it's a pig. I've seen it! If a person has a baby, it's a person.'

His wife scolds the older child: the youngest is crying. The toddler tears the *tortilla* into little pieces and places them in rows on the table.

'How could my ancestor be a monkey?' he asks.

His wife pauses. She turns to him and smiles an indulgent smile. 'Life is just a big *tortilla*.'

She loves Pablo too.

One out of Seven

It's evening and, coffee mugs in hand, we're sitting on the floor of a student's one-roomed home in Culiacan, telling ghost stories. We've just completed a sixteen-hour clinic where the queue stretched a kilometre—men, women and children with disabilities waiting, desperate for David's generous help. Still we haven't seen everyone; there'll be another big day tomorrow. A drooping candle flickers in the corner and the sounds from the slum outside slowly subside into silence. There's Fred, a young splint-maker from California, David Werner and myself.

'Lots of witches in those villages up in the Sierra,' David drawls as he stretches his legs out. 'And ghosts. Crawling with them.' His tone is super casual. 'And you shouldn't take these Mexican stories lightly either; I can vouch for lots of them myself. Used to wander those mountains way back. Maud, my donkey and I knew everyone up and down the river. Those things happened alright.'

Leaning against the concrete wall, he begins:

'There's a *pueblo* up yonder past Ajoya called Tequito[1], way into the mountains. No roads for miles. They're corn growers, but pretty much hand to mouth—not much fertile land up there. Our primary health workers used to visit Tequito once a fortnight. Pepe used to go most of the time—he'd set off on Mondays if I remember rightly.' He turns to

---

1   Village and people's names have been changed.

me. 'You remember Pepe, don't you, from Ajoya?'

'One of the health workers? The guy like a string bean who always wore that cowboy hat with the high crown?' I ask. I'd liked Pepe.

'Yeah. A real dude, but he was an ace at doctoring. Alrighty. Where was I? Now in Tequito a family by the name of Monoatl lived in a hut down by the river. I knew them well. I used to visit there, way before our primary healthcare project started up in Ajoya. There was old Ma Monoatl, a woman with a face like a brown sundial, old Pa, a scrawny old fart, and then there were seven littlies, all scrawny like their pa.

'They were pretty much the same as the other families in the *pueblo* except for the Indian surname.' David laughs. 'They're pretty well all Aztec descendants up there—of course you just have to take one look at the cheekbones—but the Monoatl's were the only ones who hadn't at some time changed to a Spanish surname.' He looks at me quizzically over his glasses. 'Silly, isn't it? If it were me, I'd be proud to have Indian ancestry.

'Anyway, one day the second son, Ramiro, got himself all steamed up over a girl. A neighbour let on that she was batting her eyelashes at another pipsqueak lad down the hill. Ramiro took off like a maniac, burst into the poor lad's home and knifed him. Killed him, then took off like a rabbit into the mountains.

'The boy hid for a few years, but eventually must have thought it safe to come home, because he moved back in with his family, and life went on. I saw him myself in the *pueblo* when I was up with Pepe, doing polio vaccinations.

'But it seems he came back too soon. A few months later a truck pulled up outside the house. Four men dressed in black with scarves over their faces slid from the truck and entered the house. They shot Ma

37

and Pa Monoatl and six kids, including Ramiro.

'All dead, except one. The seventh kid, Enrique, leapt out the window and ran.

'It must have been real easy to follow him. They just had to follow the blood trail down to the river. But Enrique dived to the bottom where the reeds were thick and breathed through a hollow reed stem for thirty minutes, all the time keeping pressure on the wound. Only then did he surface, creep quietly up the bank and slip through the trees. Then he limped north through the mountains.

'It was Pepe who stumbled upon Enrique, years later, in a *pueblo* right near the United States border. God knows why Pepe was hanging out up there—some questions I don't ask. But the kid told him the story. He kept saying to Pepe that it was the village witch, Consuela, who'd put a spell on them all, as Consuela was the mother of the murdered boy. One thing was certain. There was no way that Enrique would ever return to Tequito.

'A year went by. Then, one morning, Pepe came running into the clinic with the news that Consuela had been found in a cornfield behind Tequito with her head chopped off.'

David pauses. 'Anyone for another coffee?'

Fred and I both shake our heads, trying not to look spooked; after all, we'd both been in PROJIMO for the last two months before coming down to the city, and I, for one, had discounted the whispered stories that our next-door neighbour was a witch. I glance at Fred. He's lounging back on his cushion pretending that he hears stories like this all the time. 'No coffee after nine for me, thanks, David. I need my shut-eye,' he says in a voice a bit too loud.

With a glint in his eye, David smiles. 'I think I might have another,' he drawls, stretching as he gets to his feet. 'Coffee gives me a particularly good night's sleep.' He saunters over to the kettle.

'Now, where was I?' he murmurs from the other side of the room. I can see his outline flickering in the candlelight.

'Ah yes. Many years passed. Enrique, the seventh son, stayed away and life went on as usual in Tequito—love affairs, brawls, babies, sickness. Of course, no one had bothered to investigate the murders. The police wouldn't dare. Murders were just buried away in the collective mind.

'Then one July—I remember it. It'd been as hot as blazes and storm clouds had been gathering for days around Ajoya. Well those storm clouds burst and there was a doozie of a storm near Tequito—seven inches fell in three hours.'

David pauses as he pours his coffee. He wanders back to his cushion on the floor. 'I'd been sitting in the project garden in Ajoya, which, as you both know, is south of Tequito and up on a cliff. I remember it well —I was sitting quietly watching the piglets root around in the bougainvillea. Suddenly I heard a hideous roar—could hear it before I could see it. It was deafening! Four seconds passed then a wall of water, ten feet high and two hundred feet wide, thundered down under the cliff. In it tumbled cows, tables, trees, roofs, pigs, human bodies—and the noise! Pepe and I tore out of the garden, grabbed Jose's two horses and galloped off towards Tequito. We knew Tequito had been hit.

'Wow!' Fred sits bolt upright. 'That little stream! We were swimming in it last week!'

David looks pleased. He nods. 'It was after dark and we'd been searching along the edge of the river for survivors all afternoon.

Plodding along by torchlight, the horses were getting tired and we were exhausted. We'd found lots of animal corpses and a few human ones but nothing alive. The river was still boiling along but the debris wasn't piled so deeply now. Then we rounded a bend. Just in time! Lying in the mud was a man. He looked so mangled—I didn't think he could possibly be alive. You could see the bone through a huge gaping wound on his leg and he didn't appear to have any skin left on his chest. But he was still alive. What to do? We didn't have a stretcher. We took off our jeans and tied them to two branches, strapped him on, and walked with him to the project. The horses were so tired they followed us.

'For months Pepe and his mates looked after him at the project—damned skilled they were too, and gradually the man told them his story:

'His name was Manuel. He'd lived in Tequito with his family in the house of the murdered Monoatl's. There were seven in his family also. They'd been sitting down to lunch when they heard the roar, and the force of the water picked up his house and flung it into the torrent.

'Manuel grabbed his youngest child and clung to the little body as he was flung in the torrent. But the kid was swept away. Finally Manuel washed up three miles downstream. Pepe said Manuel was screaming every night from flashbacks.

'Manuel lost everyone in his family. Only he survived. He was the seventh.

'Ten years passed and Manuel, the seventh survivor, built another house high up from the river. He married again and had seven more children, the youngest just a baby. It was August when he noticed that storm clouds were collecting—similar to those that had caused the first disaster. His house was on the high ground, but to be extra sure he gathered up his kids and rushed them up to a little mountain hut, way up from the river. When the kids were safe in the hut, he rushed back down the mountain to his house to collect his most precious possessions. Then he heard a roar. He looked up. A flash flood was roaring down the ravine. It lightly picked up the little hut and smashed it on the rocks.

'All his children were killed but one. The seventh.' David looks up. His face seems to be wobbling in the candlelight. 'And how do I know this?' He chuckles. 'Because Manuel's surviving kid is Julio.'

'You're kidding! Little Julio—the kid with the crooked smile who makes the wooden toys in Ajoya?'

'The very one. Time to hit the sack. Another big day tomorrow.'

Fred and I say good night. I spend an uneasy night lying in jeans on the floor of a room full of mice. David sleeps in the corner like a happy sloth.

THE CHAIR

It's a ten-minute walk from Pablo's house to the project PROJIMO. At seven in the morning I leave Pablo's shady yard and walk along the dirt lane past Carmela's compound, past Pepe's mother's house covered in red bougainvillea and into the little plaza with its whitewashed church. In front of me a boy meanders bare-footed with a slingshot in his hand. A sow, its udders sagging almost to ground, looks up with her piggy eyes and collapses into dust under a tree.

A pack of dogs are fighting in front of the school and a hotchpotch of children shout and throw stones into the melee. I walk on, past the liquor store where gunshots were fired again last night, and into the main cobbled street lined with tiny shops.

'*Buenas dias, Senora*,' calls Pepita from her booth.

Ah good! She is open. I buy two sheets of paper (she sells paper by the page) and a new biro, thank her and walk on. Past the little shop selling fresh *tortillas*, past the booth selling spangled hair ornaments and perfumes, past the one selling rope, sacks of grain and plastic buckets, past the booth selling chewing gum and cheap romances, and I am at Mario's. Turn right and here is the project PROJIMO for Disabled Village Children.

It's humming. It's humming because David is here. Children with functioning and not-so-functioning bodies are squealing and laughing in the playground; groups of young people in wheelchairs are gossiping;

42

there's a screech of metal from the wheelchair-making workshop; there's hammering and sawing; a pungent smell of heated plastic for splint-making. A group of children in the grass hut are painting wooden toys. An old man on two artificial legs is learning to walk between parallel bars and a child totters past in callipers and sandals, pushing a little wooden walking frame, yelling 'Wait for me!' to a boy who is running ahead.

David's already in the clinic and, although the room is bursting with people and noise, there's all the time in the world. All year, families of children with disabilities come here, many from way over the mountains where no cars can reach. And they stay. They stay as long as they like; as long as it takes for everyone here to help them; maybe to whip up a wooden chair, a splint, a wheelchair.

I arrive at the same time as a squat woman dressed in black. She leads a mule on which sit three children. Sandwiched between number one and three is a child of about ten who I can see has athetoid cerebral palsy. How far has the mother come, I wonder? I am too far behind to help but she doesn't seem to need it. She grabs the disabled child off the mule, slings him over her shoulder and marches into the clinic followed by the two younger ones, who slide easily off the mule by themselves.

'*Ola*', the woman says with a firm smile. 'You're the boss, I suppose,' she looks up at David.

'Uh huh,' he murmurs, stroking his beard. He's smiling broadly. David loves feisty people.

'My Paolito here needs to go to school.' With that, she plonks the child holus-bolus on the plinth and sits herself down on the only plastic chair.

The child is flat on his back and looks like an upturned crab without

43

his shell. Arms and legs are flying, his back is arched and a look of terror pulls his face into a mobile grimace.

David squats down so he is level with the child. 'School, eh? So what do you think about that idea, Paolito?'

Paolito's effort to speak sends his limbs into another wild spasm and his body is arched like a banana. The gaze in his black eyes is intense. Tongue writhing, 'Iiiii ... ' he finally manages.

The mother stands up, hefts the other two bare-footed siblings onto the plinth alongside Paolito. 'He can already read,' she says proudly.

I see David's eyes widen. He draws in a breath and then nonchalantly nods as if deep in thought. Still looking at Paolito he says, 'So we just need to help you to read more, eh? And to talk more? And to sit?'

The boy's limbs fly out again. But this time it's because of excitement. His face is wreathed in a huge toothy smile as he fights to reply. 'Shhiiiii.'

David turns to the woman. 'You'll stay a while on the project while we help him?' he asks. He has seen recalcitrant tears of relief on her cheek.

She lifts her chin. 'Yes we'll stay. Of course,' she replies brusquely. 'And our mule?'

'The kids'll look after the mule. You've come at an excellent time. Tonight, we are having a feast and there'll be dancing and singing— some families are coming up on a bus from Mazatlan with children just like yours. It's fun.'

Before this trip, Paolito has never sat up; he's never been wheeled around; he's never been away from his family's one-roomed house.

Now, four days since his arrival, his sense of freedom is breath-taking; his hoarse whoops of laughter fill the compound. We see him now, arms and legs flying as his brother pushes him at a run, strapped to a wheelchair with an old torn sheet.

'Help!' shrieks his little brother who is sitting on Paolito's lap as they do a precarious wheelie in the corner. The three scream with laughter.

'*Guidado!*' yells his mother across the compound. '*Madre di Dios*! We need you alive if you want to go to school!' The other mothers notice the overwhelming gratitude on her face as she looks across at her son's happiness. They keep their counsel. She has her pride.

Pepe, the head rehab worker, has taken over the management of Paolito from David. He calls them now to his workshop. He's been fashioning a wooden chair on wooden wheels for the boy. The chair has a carefully sloped back, to allow the child to have maximum control of his head. It has a tray where his hands might have an opportunity to be able to grasp or point, and it has a footplate to hold the feet steady. The big question everyone is asking is: will it be possible for the child to communicate and use his hands, if he is positioned well enough to inhibit the spasticity? No one disagrees that he is intelligent; it is patently obvious in his eyes.

'Okay young man,' says Pepe with a grin, lifting his cowboy hat and placing it on the boy's head. 'Time for a ride in the Paolitobil!'

Paolito jerks his head up to look at Pepe's thin, towering figure and the movement throws his body into spasticity. Pepe, realising his mistake, immediately squats down to bring his face at eye level with the boy. The spasm subsides. Carefully he lifts the boy with his little body flexed and places him gently into the new chair. He rolls a few rags around the boy's shoulders and fixes them with straps. A soft pillow is placed behind his head so he doesn't hurt himself. The waist and foot straps are secured. We all hold our breath.

'Okay Paolito,' says Pepe briskly. 'Show us how you can pick up this wooden block. Take it easy. Don't try too hard, okay?'

To his side, his mother twists a scarf in her hands, her gaze riveted on the boy's hand. Pepe holds the boy's left hand firmly on the tray.

Slowly Paolito's right hand moves towards the block, the fingers extended in a sort of claw. And there! He's laughing. We're all laughing. He is holding the block. Not only is he holding it, he is releasing it; he is moving it from one side of the tray to the other.

'Bravo!' we all yell.

This time his mother doesn't hide her tears. 'He used his hand,' she whispers incredulously.

Small pictures of objects are brought and stuck to the tray. 'Can you point to the picture of the drink?' his mother asks him. 'The *tortilla*?' 'The picture of the toilet?'

Again, and again he is accurate. His mother turns to the crowd (here it is customary for everyone to watch and take part). 'See,' she crows. 'I told you he can read!'

Pepe squats down in front of Paolito, holding both hands firmly now on the tray. He points to the boy's mother. 'Who is that?' he asks.

At first there is too much grimacing, too much effort. He cannot get any sound.

'Try again,' says Pepe patiently. 'Relax and tell me who this is.'

Those burning black eyes understand well enough. 'Mmmamaa.'

Now the mother is sobbing. 'Well I guess it's time for you to go to school,' says Pepe, matter-of-fact. 'And it's smoko for me.' His voice cracks as he strides out into the yard.

The village school children paint Paolito's new chair, which now has a pommel on the tray to steady his left hand while he points with his right. They paint the chair red, orange and blue. There are flowers and pigs and a big sun with yellow rays. On the tray is the alphabet, the letters placed in the same order as on a computer. If he can master elementary spelling of words then maybe his mama can come again to PROJIMO; maybe an old computer can be found for him.

It is time for the family to return home. In the last fortnight Paolito's mother and brothers have all learnt how to help the boy to balance, to stand with support, and how to speak. They've been taught how to apply pressure to his joints to steady his wild movements, and to position him so that he has optimal use of his limbs. And it has all been fun. David has organized a donkey to take the chair. The donkey will be returned to the project later, when the farmers from her village come to market with their corn.

Everyone is out in the dirt lane to wave goodbye. The three brothers sit astride the mule, the mother walking alongside. She leads the mule and the donkey trots behind as they set off for their mountain home.

Pepe turns to David. 'I'll need to go to their village to follow up with the school as soon as I can. I may have to stay there a while ... '

David nods. 'I'm sure you'll find one teacher in the school who'll believe in the boy ... '

He sighs.

47

ISHMAEL

They brought you into the *pueblo* last night on a home-made stretcher, a three-hour walk through the Sierra and across the river. The village health worker came to the project PROJIMO for help, and together everyone was swift and adept at splinting your neck.

You'd been drinking for five days and it wasn't easy to tell if you had brain damage or were merely drunk. You certainly were quadriplegic.

They said you climbed a five-metre-high wall and fell onto your neck. Why, Ishmael?

Do you see your family hovering close, faces drawn and silent; the steady stream of awkward amigos from the *pueblo*, that shuffles past your bed?

No one cares to work today. They have no wish to talk except in huddled whispers … He won't last the night … The family can't afford the hospital …

Was it because the rich landowner didn't pay you for your work? You couldn't marry your fiancé without the money? They say that your family couldn't help. You have six brothers and sisters with stomachs to fill—three already dead, no?

Last year a knife in your back narrowly missed your spinal cord. Why, Ishmael?

Here in PROJIMO, many have damaged spines. From their wheelchairs, they'll care for you. You'll be one of them. You're young, good looking. You'll fit in okay. There are even gringos.

It could be that your fiancé will still marry you. There may be a chance—at least here in Ajoya most people see that as okay. Outside, maybe not.

You can learn to make wheelchairs. There won't be much choice to do other work. Just as your family has no choice but poverty.

*　　　*　　　*

Seven men in uniform stormed the project today waving machine guns. They grabbed a young lad and threw him against the truck, arms and legs spread-eagled. Seven guns pointed at him.

The project was crowded because the young man who fell from the wall had just died and they were putting him into a coffin. The soldiers ran through the crowd, from room to room, pistols in one hand, rifles in the other.

Children with cerebral palsy played peacefully on the swings and the men with paraplegia continued to mould the braces they were making, scarcely looking up. The women were absorbed in washing clothes from their wheelchairs and Juan de Dios whistled as he hammered the special chair he was making.

The soldiers marched the boy along the drive, hands high in the air and threw him into one of the army trucks.

They leapt onto the trucks, guns pointed skywards. Within seconds they were off, roaring down the road, around the corner and gone.

I asked what was happening.

'Nothing,' was the reply.

ANGEL

We're walking through the muddy streets of a slum in Culiacan, one pair of health workers per street, looking for children with a disability. It's not difficult to find them: there are between two and four people with a disability per street.

A while back, a wealthy benefactor donated a cottage for us to set up the project. An Australian colleague and I are working with the Mexican project team.

The team is made up of a mixture of idealistic university students and young people with disabilities such as quadriplegia, cerebral palsy and amputated limbs. We all pitch in together and the energy level is high.

Today I'm working with Paula, a sweet girl who's studying medicine. She's in love with one of the boys with quadriplegia on the project, an extremely intelligent lad, who only has movement in one hand. The two are inseparable and can be heard in the dark evenings murmuring to each other in the project yard, Jose lying on a plinth so that the two can easily kiss.

Paula and I wander down a street. It isn't long before we're directed to a squat hut. The front door is wide open and, as seems to be the custom here (privacy isn't heard of) the neighbours march in before us, announcing our presence. '*Ola, Consuela! Extranjera! Trae* Mattito!'

The woman of the house looks around and greets us easily. She's stirring something in a large pot. There are kids running everywhere, noise, smoke, and the bevy of neighbours.

Paula and I are used to this sort of scene. After explaining about our project and warning the woman that there are no promises of cure, we ask to see the little boy. A sad tenderness veils her face. She puts down the wooden spoon, carefully removes the pot from the fire, and, shouting a reprimand to a couple of youngsters, disappears into a back room. She returns with a little bundle in her arms.

'This is Mattito,' she says quietly as she places the infant on his back on an old wooden table.

Paula and I study the little boy. He's a bundle of skin and bones. His black eyes are huge in a pale face, his arms and legs, floppy. 'How old is he?' Paula asks gently.

'Two years old,' the mother replies, her large red hand caressing the boy's black curls.

'Has anyone helped you with him before now?' asks Paula carefully, as all the neighbours jostle to get a view.

A woman at the back of the crowd bustles in closer. 'I'm the grandmother,' she says with loud authority. 'Of course no one has helped! Of course the authorities turn a blind eye. What are we supposed to do, eh? Eh? How many children with polio in this street, eh? And do they do anything to stop it? Do they look after the *pequenos*? Huh! Look! We haven't even a roof—just cardboard!'

The mother ignores her mother-in-law and turns to Paula. 'I tried to get help, *Signorita,* but it is too expensive. Mattito doesn't eat. He can't move his tongue properly. I worry so much.'

'Would you mind if we take a look at him?' I ask.

'Of course! Of course!'

I pick up the little boy and sit with him on my lap, surrounded by the crowd.

Cerebral palsy. Again. So many.

There's raw sewage running down the gutter outside the house and mosquitoes are everywhere. If this brain injury isn't from malarial encephalitis, it's bound to be meningitis from dirty water or poor midwifery. This little mite has very low muscle tone and a high wailing voice.

Will he make it? Who knows?

But this is what our project is for.

After examining him, we turn to the mother. 'The project is two streets from here. There are lots of other mothers who are learning together, to help their children get stronger. We can teach you how to hold him, how to feed him, how he can learn to move a little—if that is possible … '

Paula and I stop. We can see the desperate hope on the mother's face. We have to be so careful not to raise expectations. There's no cure for cerebral palsy.

'All we can do is help Mattito to make the most of his little life.'

A mixture of emotions crosses the mother's face. She nods. 'I'll bring him,' she says simply. 'He's my little angel.'

GOING UP? GOING DOWN?

Ajahn Sobin, a Thai forest monk, has come to the village of Tequisquiapan, Mexico, from Thailand in order to introduce Buddhism into the country. It is the fifth day of our meditation retreat and we students sit on our cushions in the hall. It is evening. Ajahn walks in with measured step, reaches his seat, adjusts his yellow robe, and sits down.

There is a hush while he patiently allows us to settle. I watch the candles flickering at the little altar. Ajahn folds his hands in his lap. He speaks.

'Someti' we goi' u'. Someti' we goi' dow'.' He bursts into laughter.

What is he saying? We haven't a clue but his exuberant laughter is so infectious that we laugh with him.

After a while the laughter subsides, and, taking all the time in the world, Ajahn readjusts his robe. Satima translates into Spanish, which I find easier to understand than Ajahn's Thai English:

'Sometimes we are going up, sometimes we are going down.' She looks at Ajahn expectantly, adoringly.

'Some beee-in go dow', then they go u'.' Again he rocks with laughter, as if this is the funniest thing he's ever told us.

'Some human beings go down and then they go up,' says Satima.

'Some go u', then they go dow'. Beee-in reborn million year. Million li' ti'.'

'Some go up, then they go down. Beings are reborn again and again for millions of years. Millions of life times.'

'I pass you in huma' realm—you goi' dow' to hell, I goi' u' to heavin. We might say hello!' He giggles; his plump belly bounces. 'Start in hell realm—136 hells—col' and ho'.'

'I might pass you in the human realm this lifetime. You might be heading for hell; I might be going up to heaven this time. We might say hello as we pass each other. There are 136 cold and hot hells.' Satima finishes and looks down on us with a beatific smile, as if she is already an angel borrowed for the day.

I look around at the students next to me, squirming on their cushions. There is palpable tension.

'Then after we in ea' ho' and col' hell sufferi' we go u' to Hungry Ghost realm. Dee … si … errr in hungry ghost realm. Suffer dee … si … errrr.'

'After we have suffered in each of the 136 hells for many lifetimes we may go up to being a hungry ghost, and that is characterised by huge desire. Suffering comes from desire.'

'Then animal realm. Then u' again. Human realm. Very lucky. This one goo'.'

'The human realm is lucky, good,' puts in Satima.

'Gain merit in human realm? Ye'? Then u' we go—to jealou' heavin and up very high to *Permaloca* (goo' heavin').'

'Depending on how much merit we have accumulated in the human realm we go up firstly to the jealous heaven and finally, if we have much merit, to *permaloca* or the best heaven.'

'Stay *permaloca* hundre' thousan' year. All ni','

'You might stay in 'good' heaven for a hundred thousand years—it's nice there,' puts in Satima.

'But boring too.'

Again Ajahn is laughing

'Poor *permaloca* person. He very boring! Merit burn up in hundre' thousan' year. So dow' he go … ' He looks at me mischievously. 'Hello Li'. I goi' dow', are you goi' u'?'

'Million year all going u' and dow'—like in big circus tent. At *Permaloca* we hit the ceiling in circus tent and can't get out exce' to go dow'. In hell, suffering so big, have go u'. But who see the little door in human realm? No one. Door here. We can go to freedom through that door. No more circus tent.

'Now we fini' lesso'. Who is goi' u' and who is goi' dow' in this hall?' he asks.

He looks around at us, and his face floods with compassion.

INDIA

An Exceptional Ordinariness

Puna, India. 1983. The Aid project conference is in its second day. We are in a concrete room with large, glassless filigree windows. We sit in rows, on plastic chairs, the postures of the white-skinned participants sending out subtle messages of superiority and purpose. With the exception of the novice health workers from Kerala, black faces are impassive.

The young girls from Kerala are clustered together to one side in a gaggle of excitement, their eyes bright, smiles shy, saris rustling. And then there's the Australian, young Amanda, striding around with her long fair hair wild and tossing. She seems to be everywhere in the room, her scarlet Indian outfit and scarf flying out as she strides. Already there have been some mutterings as we drank our chai earlier.

'Only some will do the evaluation that Amanda suggests,' Rahul politely informed me. 'Maybe it is not Indian way, measuring in numbers how we do our work.' He laughed a little, very politely, those black eyes burning.

The Sydney-based director of the Aid organization sits stiffly in the middle of the front row. In his grey suit and maroon striped tie, he nurses a large clipboard. Brian, the chairman, is here too, but blended in with his neighbours in the back row. He makes no show. He has a big, bushy beard that looks as if it's never been trimmed.

The day progresses. One after the other, project leaders from all over India stand up and recount their success stories. Some have slides and we see barren fields, huge hand-dug wells and villagers handing buckets of soil one to another in long lines. We see photos of lush grapes and some other legume strung up on wires with a man in a white dhoti walking between the rows, smiling. There are chickens outside a little mud schoolroom, the door so small that adults must crawl to get inside. We see fences made of prickle bushes carried way up the mountain to a little patch of common land where the villagers could grow their tiny vulnerable seedlings safe from wandering cows.

We hear stories of attempted murder by moneylenders and henchmen, and of why primary healthcare hadn't improved the health until the villagers understood their entitlement to the Indian laws that were there to protect them. We hear tales of microcredit loan schemes and cow banks.

Now, finally, it is evening. Myna birds are pecking around outside and a spreading *shisham* tree throws black shade into the courtyard. There is a smell of Indian dusk as the air cools. Outside, car horns blare, there's a tinkle of bicycle bells and the putt-putt of a single stroke motorbike. We are back in the hall. Amanda is still moving on the sidelines, back and forth from a table full of papers and a blackboard full of figures. The last project is to be evaluated.

A very tall, thin man steps quietly onto the platform: he is the leader of a community development project from a remote part of Gujarat. He is dressed in a dazzling white tunic and pants, and black plastic sandals. His body is worn and a little stooped, his hair white and I see that his hands, those long, sensitive black hands, have known toil for a long, long time.

Gradually the room is hushed. It takes a while, as the excited chattering of the Kerala women is slow to quell.

He stands without speaking for a minute or so, looking gently into our eyes. We watch in silence. Finally he speaks.

'I have to tell you that I have failed,' he says simply. 'I have spent forty years but it did not result in success.'

He looks neither shamed, nor frightened. He quietly steps from the dais, walks down the aisle and sits down.

LOVING A WIFE

It's been a heady day: a visit in the morning to Nirid, a social forestry project for tribal Indians; then a long, long drive back to Bombay followed by a quiet stroll on the beach to watch the sunset. The beach is a wide, brown stretch of muddy sand, leading to brown shallow water. Smog hangs low and the sun smoulders, creating a diffuse purple glow. As usual, we're jolted from complacency. Quiet stroll indeed! There are men on horses at full gallop, merry-go-rounds, food stalls, vendors, children in goat-drawn carts, boats, fishermen hauling nets, families laughing, kids screaming with delight, colour, noise and a cacophony of smells from faeces to jasmine.

After stumbling through the variegated rabble, cows and traffic, we arrive at Patel's little flat just as night slides in. Exhausted, but still in one piece, we settle cross-legged on bright red cushions embroidered with little mirrors, on the white-tiled floor of Patel's tiny lounge room. Overhead a ceiling fan revolves slowly. Balding now, Patel's white hair stands like monkey grass from the sides of his face. He is perhaps eighty, a little man with a belly like a melon. Long black lashes hold his huge brown eyes in a permanent droop, belying the sharp intelligence within.

'It was an arranged marriage,' he says, his voice soft and tranquil. There's nothing in his manner to suggest the sort of tiredness we're feeling after such a long, difficult day. 'It didn't occur to us to protest.

We just accepted that our parents had wisdom and would choose well for us—after all they probably knew us far better than we knew ourselves at such a young age. We met each other twice before the wedding—of course never alone—and I was gratified to see that my new wife would be beautiful. I know that beauty should not be a significant factor in marriage but I am afraid to say that it had some importance for me when I was twenty. I must say, I was rather looking forward to more intimate communication with this lady.' His face lit up with the humour of his memory, as he bobbled his head from side to side, Indian way, to emphasize his point.

'The wedding was colourful, of course. Have you had the opportunity to visit an Indian wedding?' he asks.

We shake our heads.

'She looked exquisite, dressed in red sari, her hair piled up with jewels, her hands and fingernails painted with henna in intricate patterns, tiny feet in crafted sandals. I fell in love with her at the very sight. I guess that was the intention of the family, no?' He chuckles.

'You know, I thought it wasn't possible to love another human being more than I did that wedding night—and indeed for the first few years it was very ... ' He smiles again, an indulgent smile at his youthful self. 'Of course, you understand, the love was centred here.' He indicates his pelvis. 'It was passionate; we were on fire; I would drown in her eyes alone.'

Not in the least embarrassed, he turns to my husband. 'You can understand the circumstances, yes?'

Brian laughs. 'Of course.' He stretches out his legs.

Patel smiles. 'Then our children came.' He turns to me deferentially. 'We had five, you know.

'And soon we became enveloped in some storms, my wife and I—not, you understand, because of children. No! They were a delight to us. My wife was headstrong and young and stubborn. Even as stubborn as I. But she was still an enchantress, so it was difficult to decide to which end I was standing at any one time. She had lustrous black hair to her waist, her skin was like silk, her teeth perfect—but the way she used to hold her head—it was like this, yes?' Patel stands up, elongates his neck and lifts his chin.

'She didn't even raise her voice—but I knew! There were times when we didn't like each other at all. I wondered why she had been chosen for me. Surely my parents had made a mistake? She was so different from me; she loved adventure, pretty things. Sometimes she would even defy my own mother!' Patel pauses, eyes closed, remembering. 'Of course, I admired her defiance as much as it angered me. And always I had the problem of the loins, you know?'

He smiles wryly and stands up to stroll over to a low, intricately carved table. Musky smoke spirals up from an incense burner on the table, mingling with the hot, humid air in the room. It smells like a temple, as do the frangipani garlands that the tribal Indians placed around Patel's neck. He carefully picks up the silver-framed photograph sitting next to the joss stick and brings it over to us. A couple, side by side under a palm tree, look straight at us from serious eyes. She's dressed in a pink sari and he, a white cloth tunic and trousers. In front, two children, a girl in a white, frilled dress and a small boy in a sailor suit.

'You understand—we had no wisdom of love then. Love was only fire—boom it's alight and poof it's extinguished.' He freely indicates his genitals again as he chuckles. 'That is not to say that we did not have fun, but we each wanted our own way.

'So now learning had to start. Who was this infuriating woman who was my wife?' He looks over to me, his gaze self-effacing. I'm grinning.

'But not only that. Who was I? What was I afraid of losing if I let more of myself be known to her?'

An old toothless woman in an azure-blue sari shuffles into the room bearing a tray of cups and saucers and a large, china teapot.

'Tea?' he enquires peacefully. 'And may I introduce my aunt, Dipti? She is ten years older than I, eh?'

We stand to greet her, 'Namaste,' hands together to our chins. She smiles gently and returns our greeting.

'Namaste.'

Patel sits, at ease with the slowness and quiet as his aunt pours the tea, the only sound to disturb the restfulness. He hands the cups to us and sips his own for a while, the beat of the ceiling fan punctuating the stillness.

'It was a very long journey, all the time trying to chase this elusive condition, love.' He carefully places the cup on the saucer and smiles at the old woman. 'It's funny, yes, how we play these little games with ourselves to mask our fear of giving and receiving love? So much ego in our way.

'So we smashed ego,' he indicated with his fist. 'And each decade that moved past—and we had six decades of marriage you know—we smashed more.

'As I said, at first it was desire. And tangled up in our desire was the wish—quite unconscious you know—to own the other. She and I both entered into this mistake.

'Then I started to dedicate all my time to work and my priorities were in entirely the wrong place. You understand, I was seduced by my wish to succeed and partially this was in order to provide for my family. An elemental need for a man. Also, of course, I enjoyed feeding my ego in this way. I liked and yet despised my wife's dependence on me. She— well she did not like being in a dependent position either. But I must say that our society colludes to keep us thinking along these lines.

'But, as we find out in time, it is not possible for a seed of love to take root on a speedway. Love enjoys time that slowly revolves right here. Luckily, it was she, in her wisdom, who opened my eyes. So, I sold our large house for this tiny one, so that circumstances would be right for the seed to grow roots.

'We moved on, of course, to more subtle obstacles. How we clung to the identities we had fabricated for ourselves! How we clung to a life stimulated by outside events! We had terror of getting too close.' Again Patel closes his eyes. 'I remember one day we were making love. She sensed that I was fearing intimacy. She said to me,

'Come in! The water's beautiful. I am loving all of you. There is nothing to fear.'

He smiles. Brian and I look at each other.

'You know, we worked for six decades.' He laughs. 'We wished to love only some of the package. And so we become old. And maybe some wisdom has crept in, little by little, so to speak.

'I believe that we know it now, but who knows if that also is illusion?' He chuckles. 'I am sensing that I love my wife very deeply. We are true friends, she and I. She has grey hair, lines on her face, her feet are hard underneath. Sometimes in bed she snores. And I love her.

'An amusing journey we all have the good fortune to make, eh?' He smiles again, folding his arms peacefully in his lap.

'Where is your wife now?' I venture.

'She is in Canada for one year, to help our daughter with our grandchildren. But that is quite well.' The inflection of his voice rises endearingly. 'Next year she will be home again. Separation makes no difference. No difference at all.'

He stands and shuffles across the room in his silver slippers to show us to the bedroom he's vacated for us. On the dresser by the bed is a photo. A beautiful old woman with long grey hair smiling at a little bald man with a watermelon paunch.

THE STRANGE STATE OF BABILU'S MIND

Ah, Liz! Come in! Share a soft Indian dusk with me. It is my custom to do this each evening and I am most happy that you join me. Do be seated—that swinging seat with the canopy will be most comfortable for you. And Augustine, you might like the red chair? Fresh lime juice for you? It is good to drink after a hot day, no?

I must get comfortable also. I like to sit cross-legged even if I have more than seventy years. Indian custom of course. There.

Now let me share some sentimental rambling. It is all from the heart, you know. I can't help it. I am so very happy! These days, even when I feel a little angry or a little sad, I am happy. Take this morning. What should I have been doing? I should have been discussing the seed-dibbling project on the far hillside with Sanje. But where was I? Quite joyful with a little thing. Playtime with my dogs, Krishna and Parvati. I am captivated by the depth of beauty in their eyes.

Two hours disappeared like that. Looking into their faces and seeing such beauty of spirit. I was running around this courtyard with them, and no one here to watch me, and no guilt attached whatsoever. Who would have thought to find happiness in such a simple way? In your country is such exuberance commonplace?

Krishna! Parvati! Come, you beauties! You see the eyes? They are an old Indian hunting-breed of dog, you know. You may not have heard of them in Australia, but such goodness, their nature. I couldn't help all this sunniness rising up.

Sometimes I look at myself and wonder. 'Babilu,' I say, 'to what dark place did all that unhappiness fly? All that earnestness as a young man? To Bombay?'

But of course I am happy. Look at this place! This is beauty, is it not? These mountains. The greenness.

But there is a little chill from the breeze—do you wish for a shawl? Good, good!

All comes from our permaculture endeavours. And that came from your country, Liz. Such a difference it has made from the barrenness that was here before. When we came here, we dug wells—very deep, but always dry. And now water in each well only six feet from the surface. All from copying nature. Augustine, have you visited the trees that you planted—when was it? Ten years ago? Remember making little saucers on the dry hillside to catch the rain? You can see the trees from here, behind the solar panels on that hill. How tall they are!

Hear the children laughing. Who could harbour sadness when listening all day to such sounds?

I am happy that you visited our school this afternoon—the school for the learning of joy. I see from your smiles that it affected you very well. I expect Amita told you about these very children. They are from the poorest village families, those who would have had no chance to be educated. Not even first grade.

Let us be quiet for a while ... Listen ...

Laughter. That is a light-hearted sound—a good sound. We give them a gift of their childhood. That is what we're hearing—innocence. Still you smile! This is what such sound does to you.

Can I get you more juice? No? An Indian sweet, perhaps?

Where was I? Oh, yes. Happiness. Even this building brings me happiness. You like it, no? We liked to have it curving, in keeping with tradition, the mud walls painted white. The red and green design around the doors and windows are of the tribal colours from this district. And of course, the thatch—a foible of mine, a little weakness.

Let me tell you a story. Those tribal women in the village micro-banking scheme, the Women's Cooperative, the ones you met today in the compound. There are four thousand cooperatives now in the Timbuctu district. They have just completed building their first little centre. You are invited to tomorrow's opening ceremony—and the painting not yet dry. What gaudy colours they have chosen! I shudder in my sleep. They are thrilled—saved every rupee, piece by piece, created their bank, week by week, year by year. From nothing.

I am so proud for them! They call me over one morning and say:

'Babilu, we will have a concrete building. Steel roof with proper tiles. Not some crazy building but that flies away when the wind blows.'

I laughed with them. You see; they want a structure to be strong and to last many years. And I? I love the thatch. I admire beauty. Listen! You hear that music? It is a Vedanta chant. It sings in the heart. I like to hear it as the sun sets over that mountain after the heat. The evenings are gentle and it is the time to sit quietly and breathe.

The happiness comes, I am believing, from many, many years of Vedanta. Every morning I practise yoga, and so I have come to an understanding.

A life is such a tiny speck in the vast time that is the universe.

Oh, but I talk too much. Like an old man. And that I am, of course. Tell me, did you buy some organic millet? You did? Good. It will make you excellent porridge.

69

MHAISAL

With garlands around our necks, Brian and I sit cross-legged on a wooden dais in a little village hall in Mhaisal. Our knees poke skywards like signposts. On the floor below us are the erstwhile *Dalits*[2], also cross-legged. The men sit on one side, the women on the other, separated by an aisle. A hundred clear-eyed faces look up at us. Backs are straight; there's a vibrancy in the air that feels like Spring sunshine.

The introductory speech is over and now it's time for Brian and I to ask questions. Brian is silent for a moment before he asks, 'When Community Aid Abroad suggested giving you a loan to set up a small business, why did you decide to grow grapes?'

Immediately a number of hands shoot up and a young girl jumps to her feet. Black-eyed and olive-skinned, she is beautiful. With a confident toss of her head she starts to speak. It's a long story and everyone smiles and nods as she tells it in her language. Our interpreter translates: 'Before Caa came, we worked many, many hours every day. Very hard work, breaking rocks or working in the fields for the *Brahmins*. Women

---

2   Szczeoabski, Kallie. *Who are the Dalits?* ThoughtCO, 2020, Feb 04.
    Dalits / Harijans / the 'Untouchables' were the lowest caste in India. The cast system was constitutionally banned in 1950, but it was still prevalent in the 1980s in the rural areas. The word "*Dalit*," meaning "oppressed" or "broken," is the name members of this group gave themselves in the 1930s. They were denied the right to enter temples, the children were denied schooling; they were not allowed to use the village well, use public transport or choose their occupation.

and men, and children too. All of us working. We got very little money, and there was lots of fighting.' She looks happily over at the men and points.

I look at the men. They are not cowered by the shaming. They look as proud as she does.

She continues, her voice high like a blackbird. 'Caa decided that it would be best if we women ran the project as the men were spending our money on alcohol, getting drunk and violent.' Again she threw an easy look over to the men, who nodded. 'Caa had been teaching us women about how to save with microcredit. They trusted us because they knew we needed to have food for our children; we wanted our children to live in a house; we wanted our children to go to school.'

The women are all nodding.

'We thought a lot and finally decided that we wanted to grow grapes on the piece of land bought by the loan. Not another vegetable. Grapes. Because only the *Brahmins* are allowed to grow grapes. The *Brahmins* are the most respected caste—the top. We wanted everyone to see that we *Dalits* are as good as the *Brahmins*.'

She sat down, looking pleased with herself. Now it was my turn. 'What did the people from the other castes do when they heard you wanted to grow grapes?'

Now a man shot up his hand. He stood up. 'They laughed,' he said. 'They were sure we couldn't do it. That made us even more determined. We planted the vines and fertilized and irrigated them. We made sure there were no weeds. We built trellises to hold them when they grew. We did all this by ourselves with the money from the loan. Still everyone in the village avoided us and laughed. But the vines grew. Two years later they produced grapes.

'The vines were so big compared to the ones belonging to the *Brahmins*, and the grapes so lush and abundant that the trellises started to collapse. We had no more money to strengthen the trellises.'

The man looked around. Everyone was nodding.

'We didn't know what to do: it looked like we were going to lose the crops after all. It was there for all to see: the trellises were breaking and we were going to lose our crop. We could see it. The villagers walking by could see it.

'And then a miracle happened. We woke early. We were so unhappy! We looked out of our huts, and there were hundreds of villagers— hundreds! *Brahmins* and other castes, all out there propping up our trellises. The whole village saved our grapes! They respected us so much that they did that!'

I looked around. Happiness gushed from a hundred or so faces below.

The man sat down.

'What did you do with the money from the grapes?' asked Brian, the smile on his face almost splitting it in two. He loved these stories of success.

Now fifty hands were raised. They were so eager to tell their story that they looked like they'd burst from the joy of it.

'We bought saris,' said an old woman struggling to stand up from the floor.

I was surprised. 'Saris? Not food?'

Now the women seemed to grow taller; now I noticed the wonderful colours in the room. The women looked like birds of paradise. 'Until that time we each had only one sari. With our work it would get dirty and worn. When it was washed we were naked and had to stay in our hut while it dried. Now we have two, and we know we look as good as the other women in the village. We can hold our heads up!' Her gaze was direct and full of pride. 'We grew more grapes with the money as well, and we saved. Now our children go to school. Now we have food.' She looked at me. 'Now we can walk down the street on the same side as everyone else.'

Brian turned to the men. 'Now that your wives are independently earning money, how is it for you? Do you feel resentful of them?'

A young man in the third row stood up. 'At first we felt angry with our women and there were fights. We were used to being the boss,' he said with an ingenuous smile. 'But before long we realized we were happy. We men don't drink alcohol very much now. We don't fight now.'

I was astonished. I looked across to the women to see if this was actually true for them. Immediately a young woman stood up. 'It's true,' she shrilled, 'the equality has made our families content.'

Now everyone was nodding.

I looked across. Brian reached out and held my hand.

AUSTRALIA

THE HOWLING

It seems the walls themselves are oozing defeat as I walk bare-foot across the faded linoleum. I switch on lights as I go, listening to my footsteps echoing down the long passage. The silence is loud. Along the dirt road outside a dog howls into the night. Like a wild cry for help, the sound collects up other howls from dusty back yards, and soon the screaming mass hurls itself on my barred windows.

I wander into the empty lounge room with a small photo in my hand. 'First, House,' I find myself saying out loud, almost jumping in fright from the suddenness of it. 'Let me introduce my Brian. His picture goes here, smack in the middle of the mucky wall. Hi Brian! Calling Brian—are you receiving me? It's your darling wife. All alone. Far, far from you. With the smell of cabbage and no phone.'

I'm being silly and don't seem able to stop myself, especially as angry shouts and a shriek shoot out from the night like a spear. I look around. The room's too big. No furniture. I feel swallowed up by the emptiness of it.

'Sorry, Brian.' I hear my voice getting higher now. It seems to bounce around the room. 'You're probably sitting in your armchair by the fire reading The Financial Times, actually, but here you're looking a bit lost with all the graffiti and no chairs or anything. But I do have light—the night's thick black out there.'

I pull another small photo and some blue-tack from my pocket. 'Okay then, House, may I present Jo. She's my eldest daughter and she's going in the middle of that wall—the green one with the purple smears on it. And here is my youngest daughter, Francesca, who goes on the yellow wall.'

I push the photos in place and stop. I'm being ridiculous. The tiny photos look like they've shrunk into themselves.

I stand; stare at them. The silence is winning; the house is a yawning hole that sucks sound. I shoot a look at the un-curtained window and the black slit of night. Wildflowers. Huge armfuls of them. I'll find a jar for them. That'll fill up the rooms. But the thought is loud in the room and I can see its white skin. And maybe there's a chair I can find at the dump? I walk to the kitchen, fast now, to make myself a cup of coffee. My kaftan is hung over the window, a pseudo-safe curtain; there's a table and a plastic chair.

The kettle fills slowly as orange water trickles from the tap. A red stain, like blood, is scribbled down the porcelain sink: the washer needs changing. I look up. Nine fifteen. The kitchen clock is actually ticking and telling the time—maybe the right time, with ticks that are slow and even. I flick on the kettle and take the only cup out of the cupboard. Outside, a car roars past with no muffler and squealing tyres as it takes the gravelly corner too fast. A little cloud of remnant red dust floats in the window.

'Well, House,' I say out loud again as I sit down with the coffee. 'How about some music?'

I stand up; turn the cracked knob of the old radio on the shelf. A country and western song pounces out like a bunch of tin lids. I sink back into my chair. Men's music; this country's music; not my music.

Slowly I sip the coffee and watch the song flatten the silence. Tomorrow I'll hold a class for the health workers. I try running my mind over the content of the lesson. Yes, it'll be fine. I can really help, can't I? The coffee tastes of metal.

The clock ticks on. Nine twenty five. I could go to bed now, couldn't I? It's not too early. I stand up to take my cup to the sink and pause. There's an acrid smell.

Smoke.

Burning rubber tyres? Petrol sniffers? Can I see? Carefully I move the kaftan to the side and peer out. Damn the window bars. Oh yes! A fire alright—a big one. The school?

Quickly I pull the kaftan over the window again, my heart thumping.

Don't be stupid! But there were two buildings in flames last week. Is it rubber tyres?

I take a deep breath. No point getting my knickers in a knot. I'm perfectly safe here. I check the door bolt in the kitchen. Just one bolt. Just one door for the whole house. I turn.

'Yeah!' I say, my voice sounding too loud. 'No furniture. Yeah! Bars on windows and only one door at the other end of the house from the bedroom. Yeah! Yeah! Yeah! Okay House. Time for bed. Big day tomorrow in the clinic. I should stop talking to myself.'

I make my way back through the house, turn off the kitchen light, the lounge light, passage light and enter the bedroom where my swag lies on the floor in the silence. The bedroom curtains don't meet in the middle. Frowning, I find a safety pin and pin them together, unroll my sleeping bag and check again the position of the yellow button on the wall, the button to set off the rape alarm on the outside wall of the house. Carefully I place my pencil torch beside the mattress, turn off the light, and struggle in the dark to take off my jeans and pull on my pyjamas.

'Goodnight, Liz,' I whisper as I wriggle into the sleeping bag. 'Sweet dreams. And no, they won't burn the house down with me in it. Of course they won't.'

Surprisingly, I'm quickly asleep—a deep, sweet sleep. It's 2.30 when I wake up, my heart banging in my chest. It's dark—sickening, black dark. I feel up the wall for the yellow button and freeze. Just outside the window, just above my head, there's whispering.

Jemmying the bars at the window ...

Oh no! Not here! Get out of here! Yes that's right. Shush! Get your jeans on. Crawl down the passage, through the lounge. Find the door in the kitchen. What if they're waiting outside? The woman from the store had her head smashed in by an iron bar last week.

Open it.

Now! Run!

The resident doctor opens his door with a yawn, pulling a cashmere dressing gown over his night attire. 'What's the matter with you?' he mutters, squinting down at the volunteer physiotherapist from over the road.

'Youths. They tried to get into my bedroom.' I force a laugh. I'm shivering.

'You've got a rape alarm, haven't you?' His college accent squeezes out the word 'rape' as he looks down at me in irritation. He absently runs a hand through tousled, black hair and yawns again.

I feel my mouth tighten; say nothing. I notice that his little paunch makes the soft dressing gown lift at the front.

'Oh, hell! You'd better come in.' he mumbles. 'Sleep on the sofa. There's a blanket in the trunk in the corner. I'm going back to bed.'

I slink in to the brightly lit, well-furnished room, and stare after him as he wanders off towards his bedroom.

'You'll have to toughen up if you're going to survive here,' he says over his shoulder as he closes the bedroom door.

I sit down. In the street the dogs are howling again.

CALLING COUNTRY

'Stop pissin' in my fuckin' bottle!'

'Fuck off! You find your own fuckin' bottle!'

'Ay! Stop that! There's one bottle between the two of youse, okay?' Maureen's grinning. She glances in the rear vision mirror at Charlie and Snowy in the back seat of the Toyota, their black bush hats firmly on their heads. 'Not long to your country, ay. That eagle rock comin' up soon,' she croons.

She turns to Anthony. 'We always pull up at that jump-up at the end there,' she says. 'They'll need to stretch their legs. I'll take the drivin' after that.'

Anthony nods, his eyes focused on the corrugated road. A sweet smell of urine wafts through the car.

Maureen hums to herself as she rummages in a bag. 'Let's have music!' she says as she slides a disc of country and western into the recorder. 'What sort of music do ya like?'' she asks Anthony with studied casualness.

He hesitates. 'Classical actually.'

With a dismissive flick, Maureen turns up the country and western to top volume. 'Not long to ya country now, old men,' she shouts above the din.

Charlie and Snowy have moved as far away from each other as the seat allows, their little bags of possessions sitting on their laps. They're each squinting out at the glare of spear grass that covers the red sand.

'We don't do more than 75 k's an hour on these roads,' Maureen continues nonchalantly. 'Ya not used to driving Toyotas up 'ere, are ya?' She raises an eyebrow.

Anthony stiffens. 'Well I actually have a Nissan of my own in Adelaide,' he says, slowly easing off the accelerator. 'And before nursing I was an ambulance driver.'

'City driver, eh?' With a snort, Maureen turns to look out the side window. 'That arsehole Lillyskin tried it on me once on that track out of Fitzroy. Stupid idiot cruising along at 100 k's an hour. One slip and you roll. So I just let 'im be. Bide me time, that's the way. The smart-arse swerved to miss a snake and I tell 'im, "That's it. Pull over. Get out." And I left 'im there. Stupid bastard.'

She laughs. 'You want a lolly, love?'

Anthony shakes his head and continues driving steadily along the centre of the track.

Maureen shrugs. She glances again into the back seat. 'Them old men don't believe we're taking 'em to country. Don't believe nothin'.'

Her voice rises. 'How could they believe in anythin' eh? Been so long stuck in them fuckin' white hostels back in town, they almost fossilised. Bloody sterile buildings with fuckin' bureaucrats hoverin' in every fuckin' corner and no spear grass in sight.

'And all the while their country pullin' inside ... pullin' and pullin' ... 'Course you wouldn't understand.'

Shooting a look at Anthony, she says, 'And you better not mind my language, 'cos that's 'ow it fuckin' is. A fuckin' nightmare—a white fuckin' nightmare.'

She sniffs. Anthony's gaze is steady. Still on the road.

'Could be I'm with one o' them white bureaucrats right now in this car, eh?' The hard edge of her laughter jars as she takes out a cigarette, lights it, and slowly blows smoke over the windshield.

She shrugs. 'Just pullin' ya leg.'

She takes another drag, gazes out the side window. The rocky outcrop is more obvious now, its red face shining in the sun. Grassland is stretching to the horizon. 'Them old fellas don't believe nothin' no more. Just fuckin' cryin' for country.'

Pinching the end of the cigarette with her fingers Maureen chucks the butt out the window, and yells, 'Nearly there!'

Curled in their respective corners, the two old men give no indication of having heard. Outside, heat shimmers in a white sky.

'Right. Pull up 'ere. Yeah. Get the car under that shade.'

'We'll help youse out now,' she says to the two bent figures in the back. 'Let ya'selves have a nice stretch.' She turns to Anthony. 'You get Snowy. I'll do Charlie.'

It's clear that Charlie's legs aren't behaving too well and that he's shamed about the stain on the crotch of his pants. Suddenly Maureen is gentle. 'That's the way,' she says quietly as she steadies him. 'Just put one hand here and one hand there and you can get out by ya'self.' She flicks a warning glance at Anthony as he helps extricate Snowy.

She turns back to Charlie. Slowly the old man straightens and takes the long stick offered. He totters up the rise.

'Let 'im be,' Maureen warns quietly as Anthony starts after him.

They watch as Charlie struggles to the top. They watch him pause, his rheumy fingers fumbling at the old bush hat as he squints out across the plain. Spear grass stretches out and a smoke haze wavers on the horizon.

Suddenly a wail surges out and tears pour down the old man's leathery cheeks.

'Aaaaaaaaiiiiiii … aaaaaiuuuuueeeeeee … aaaaaaaiiiiiiiiiiiiii … aiiieeeueeeeeee … '

Maureen jolts forward. 'Hey! Charlie! What's all that wailin'?' she yells as she scrambles up the slope.

At the top she stands beside him, panting. Slowly her gaze follows Charlie's as his keening continues, the sound reaching way out across his country. And finally there's silence, a deep, deep silence filled with the quiet drone of flies.

'Yeah, Charlie. It's ya country,' she whispers.

Her face crumples as she gently touches his shoulder, her face averted from his tears. 'We're moving on now, Uncle,' she mutters, as tears trickle down her cheeks also, the tragedy of it so immense that she stumbles as they start to descend.

In a voice as hard as an ants' nest she turns to Anthony. 'Get that other fella back in and we'll be going. No point them two getting too happy. They can only stay a fortnight in their country. Then they goin' back to the hostel. White bureaucrat orders.'

The driver winces at the pure hatred directed at him.

Maureen hands him some water. ''Ere love. Drink this. You can get dry up 'ere if you're not careful.'

THE TEACHING

He's an old man. Or is he? Maybe age has a different meaning here in Pitjantjatjara country.

He's working quietly, fashioning a *coolamon*, sitting cross-legged in the black stripes of shade, his stick thighs and calloused feet seeming comfortable with the desert sand. Tall red gums stand motionless overhead, and afar off there is an occasional screech of corellas.

I'm aware of the silence. It's a silence that's broken with the movement of his knife. Chip. Chip. Chip, chip, chip.

We stand for what feels like a good ten minutes at the edge of the clearing, waiting for his invitation. At last he beckons my friend forward. She crouches in front of him—not too close: she knows about respect.

With the pink pad of his slender black finger, he shows her his story on the wood. It's long. I think it's a snake. He tells it in Pitjantjatjara—not all at once as if he had an audience, but with deep pauses, as if the two of them are wrapped in a secret. She's his adopted daughter—or is it granddaughter? This young white woman who has so much to learn, and he so patient with his teaching.

All the while I stand and watch, she repeating, he talking very softly, almost a mumble. No need to shout a sacred story in such a place where the trees stand silently in the glare and the spaces stretch. Watching her, she seems gently humble, her head bent in deference as she follows that bent finger moving over the wood.

There isn't a beginning or an end to the story that I can tell. Here we're in something vast that stretches and circles. Not what I would call 'time'. He doesn't seem to live in our sort of time—or space, for that matter. He isn't concerned that night is coming on and we have a long walk back to Ernabella—maybe two hours. Already the sky is red behind the trees and the clearing soft in shadow, the forest dark.

Finally, my friend stands up, thanks him. I mutter 'thank you', from where I stand. He doesn't seem to acknowledge our thanks, or our parting. Just sits there comfortably on the earth as the sun goes down.

Did we do this to them? Did we take their land, take their culture, take their children, their ancestors, their language, their place, their food, their animals, their trees, their stars? De-humanise them? Herd them into gulags?

Kill them … ?

Yes. We did.

IN THE LISTENING

'Hello Dolly!' Jenny says. 'How are you today? I've brought you a brace for your floppy foot and a tripod to help you to walk. They came today on the plane from Darwin!'

Jenny squats down in front of Dolly's little *wiltja*[3] looking away to keep her nervousness from showing. This is scary. Has she remembered all the cultural protocol? Don't look anyone in the eye. Don't ask questions. Don't assume ...

She looks around. Don't assume? But how can this old lady live like this? The *wiltja*—just sticks and grass! Rubbish everywhere! Where—and how on earth—does she take a crap? She can only hitch herself around on her bottom! And the dogs! Three of them. They've probably got fleas. And who does her washing?

Oh yes! She can help! She can give Dolly a whole new life!

---

3   Wikepedia: *Wiltjas* are shelters made by Aboriginal Australian peoples. They are temporary dwellings, and are abandoned and rebuilt rather than maintained. Open and semi-circular, *wiltjas* are meant primarily as a defence against the heat of the sun, and are not an effective shelter from rain. 2021

'I've got you a pair of leather sandals,' she says, her confidence mounting a little. 'The brace holds your foot up. So it doesn't drag. And the sandals'll be cooler than boots. The tripod's going to steady you. And I've organised for the carpenter to come and make you some parallel bars so you can learn to walk. I'm going to instruct the health worker to help you do it.'

Jenny turns expectantly to Doreen. 'Can you translate that please?'

Doreen stands back diffidently, turns side on, and quickly repeats Jenny's speech in Pitjantjatjara. Then she walks off.

Jenny now feels uncomfortable. Is Doreen, Dolly's daughter in law or something? In laws aren't allowed to speak to each other? Is that it?

She tries the sandals on Dolly's bare feet, fits the brace and helps Dolly to stand up, placing the tripod in her good hand.

'There!' she says loudly. 'See! I told you that you could learn to stand and walk! It just takes practice. Look! I'll support you on your bad side and you lean on the tripod. There you go!'

She watches as Dolly's face changes.

Is it bemused? Or scared? Excited? Or is Dolly humouring her.

Are they all humouring her?

'See?'

By then two other women have strolled up. They laugh and throw remarks. Jenny doesn't understand the language but from the tone she thinks it's a tease. She smiles.

'Look!' she says theatrically. 'We can walk to that plastic chair and then you can sit down. Okay?'

It's five steps away and Dolly manages it with Jenny's support. She's panting and points to her *wiltja*.

Does she want to go back? The dogs have wandered over and flop at her feet.

'She wants her drink of water!' one of the spectators yells, laughing.

Jenny scuttles back to the *wiltja*, picks up a jam jar of water and brings it to Dolly. Dolly takes it and yells something back to the women.

'She says leave her there in the chair. She's had enough for today.' All the women laugh.

Jenny moves slowly from community to community, driving over red earth, earth that starts to speak to her. Over a rise, there's a sea of flowers as far as the horizon and only she to witness the quiet of it. Or enormous slabs of red granite. Wedge-tail eagles soar on thermals and the flute duet of butcherbirds awaken her. There's sudden rain and mud. She tastes bush tomato, wild fig, honey ants. Gradually over months she's swallowed whole by the night sky, and opened to desert silence like a child's hand.

And along the way she's realizing the awe and terror of not knowing. And again, not knowing.

And again.

Until she begins to see—bit by bit. As if she'd been swimming above water all her life, to suddenly discover what it is to plunge with snorkel and mask, wide-eyed with astonishment, into the depths of another way to be. Embracing what is under; what is inside—a world so beautiful, so intelligent … and so alien. She's dreamt of this, longed for it.

And yet she's shocked. What has she been doing all her life? Where, in her Western culture, were there lessons about connection to every single form—every person, every living and inanimate being? Every happening? Every rock. Every piece of land. Every ancestor.

How much has she been indoctrinated into blindness? Who said Dolly—or any of these people with disability—need to play victim in order for she, Jenny, to become saviour? Who said her dominating culture was superior? Look how it has destroyed the earth, the rivers, polluted the sea, the sky!

The shocks pile up on each other.

Bit by bit.

The teaching is not always patient—in either direction. Not always gentle.

But gradually Jenny is seeing into the not doing. The not doing. And deep listening itself becomes the teacher; assumptions torn out like teeth. A different 'giving' growing. Humble. Easy.

Five months pass. Driving alone, Jenny calls in to an outstation to give Auntie K a massage. She has been told that the old lady is tired out, caring for children from one of the communities. There are twelve of them at the moment—petrol sniffers who'd been relentlessly destroying their brains—so much easier, the children think, to numb out, than face the hopelessness of cultural genocide. Auntie K has been restoring their souls by teaching them lore out here in Country.

There's no guilt in Jenny's touch now as she massages Auntie K. The enormity of what her culture did to these people, sweeping through her again and again during the first months, like desert dust storms, has lessened. It has been raw. But now, slowly the guilt, the desperate need to redeem, to fix, transforms into humility.

She doesn't need recognition and there's no hurry. She doesn't even give names to days any more—not Monday-to-Friday names. A day becomes memorable by knowing that what is happening is exactly what should be happening right now.

At the far end of the Lands, Jenny picks up a bunch of old people, gives them a lift out to their *wiltjas* in the desert.

'Little bit long way,' they describe the distance, laughing with her as they all climb into the Toyota.

This time, the 'little bit long way' is about two hours, a rollicking journey with babies, children and old folk jammed together, laughing and chattering. They hand around a char-grilled goanna to munch on. Jenny eats her portion, smiling. As they pass through red country she listens to the women telling stories to the little ones, sensing that the stories weave each landmark to others far and near. They weave in ancestors, astronomy, and a sense of belonging to kin, land and animals.

The old women return another day on the back of a truck. Jenny massages them one by one, realizing how her old definition of 'work' has changed. The boundary between it and play has disappeared. The old women discard their clothes and wriggle onto the dirt floor of the shed and Jenny kneads rolls of fat with oil. Every now and then the women hoot with laughter, grab her hand and move it to the 'correct' spot, in hysterics at her lack of knowledge. At the end of the day Jenny sits on the dirt under a sky whirling with stars.

She is invited to a little women's ceremony out in the desert, the women naked to the waist and striped in ochre. For hours she sits on the sand as they chant.

This is a different sort of happiness. She sits under a tree with a bunch of elders; telling stories, listening. She tells of her surprise that two thousand white people come to the Lands each year to give 'advice' on how the First Nation people should live. She recounts her time in India; about how tribal people created change for themselves by taking back their power. She expresses sadness because the Pitjantjatjara elderly folk are being placed in homes far from country, and she asks how they might bring their old people home. She talks of her awe of the ngankari[4]—would it be possible for traditional and white doctors to work together in partnership? To help their sick children—so many with pneumonia, so many dying?

Having no answers. Speaking of awe ...

It's six months since Jenny has seen Dolly.

In a green floral dress, the old lady sits barefooted outside her *wiltja*, two dogs beside her. There's a jar of water, a plate of food; a little fire crackles its sharp language of warmth and hospitality.

Jenny smiles as she approaches the circle. 'Palya', she says.

Dolly looks up. She pats the ground beside her.

Jenny sits, easy with the quiet, and gazes around. She notices the splint and sandal decorating a large bush near the *wiltja*. There's no sign of the tripod.

After a while she indicates a jar nearby. 'You been noodling?' she asks Dolly in language.

---

4   Wikipedia: *Ngangkari* are the traditional healers of the Anangu, the Aboriginal peoples who live mostly in the Anangu Pitjantjatjara Yankunytjatjara (APY Lands) of South Australia and the Western Desert region ... *Ngangkari* have been part of Aboriginal culture for thousands of years, and attend to the physical and psychic health of Anangu. 2021.

Dolly's smile broadens. '*Uwa.*' With her good hand she passes Jenny a jar of tailings from the nearby Mintabi opal mine, an invitation to join in her search for opal chips. Chatting companionably, they noodle side-by-side for an hour or so.

Suddenly Dolly lets out a piercing yell. 'Ay! Doreen! You mob goin' Ernabella? I got to sit down with Shirley!'

A woman across the square yells back.

Half an hour later a car pulls up, a bunch of women pick Dolly up and bundle her into the front seat. Jenny stands, dusting off her skirt and Dolly waves cheerily as the car disappears in a cloud of red dust.

Ambling back to the clinic, Jenny returns the friendly waves from people sitting outside their houses.

Her beginning has begun. It's her own people with whom she now needs to talk—deeply.

SUDAN

WHISTLING IN SUDAN

We're hurtling across the burning desert sands in Eastern Sudan in a troopie between the camp for Tigrayan refugees and the Aussie compound. Full throttle, the nurses are singing:

Always look on the bright side of life
Life's a piece of shit
When you look at it,
Life's a laugh and death's a joke, it's true ...

The camp doctor sits in the corner, not amused, and Heshe, the Tigrayan driver, eyes ahead, is smiling.

'Join in, Heshe! Join in!' calls Marguerite from behind.

Heshe's smile flickers. I catch his eye in the rear vision mirror. Tolerance? Humour? Bewilderment? 'I cannot sing,' he says.

Outside, the bleached sand stretches flat as far as the horizon in every direction. We are driving along a faint track, not a road.

'Do you want to hear a funny story?' Anne is grinning.

'Sure!' we shout above the din of the old Toyota.

We laugh as she puts on her storytelling face. We need this ritual, this unwinding time after twelve hours of work. We need our humour.

'Well it happened this morning before any translators arrived. This woman came into the ward for a check-up. She had on a gorgeous red floral dress and she looked about eight months pregnant. So, I sat her down on one of the matting beds and told her I'd be back in a minute.

'There was an emergency at the other end of the ward—can't remember what, but we were dealing with that when all of a sudden I heard one hell of a ruckus from down where I'd left the pregnant woman. There she was in her fabulous dress writhing around on the dirt floor and it looked like she was going to pull the matting wall down in one fell swoop. I took one look at her—Crikey! Full-on labour!

'A couple of other women helped me get her onto the bed again. We whipped a screen around her and I lifted her dress to examine her. All hell broke loose! She started screaming and writhing and struggling. Hells bells! What to do? I ran full pelt into ward B and grabbed Josie and Birikti. 'Quick!' I yelled. 'There's a baby on the way and she won't let me examine her!'

'Birikti grabbed Mabaret—you know, the new female translator—and we tore back to Ward A. Mabaret hurried into the cubicle and explained to the woman that we had to lift her dress to see how her labour was progressing, but, quick as a flash, Mabaret was out of there.

'Lady have scorpion bite,' she said. 'Not married. Not pregnant.'

'My mouth fell open. Sure enough, the woman's stomach was as flat as a flounder. I came out of the cubicle and looked across and there was the pregnant lady in the next bed, in the same dress. And the lady next to her had the same dress on too!

'I felt such a fool! But they just laughed and laughed. It made their day. The story'll probably go all over the camp, and I'll be the donkey.' Anne's eyes were twinkling.

'Anyway, we got a shot of pain relief for the scorpion woman and by then the pregnant woman had vamoosed—probably in fear of her life. But, do you know, we had eight women in the same dress that morning. They must have had one bolt of material for all of them. Could be it was in the last batch of cast-offs from Red Cross last week.'

We all laugh. 'Well. In my ward, they're much better-dressed,' pipes up Marguerite. She bursts into a very off-key song:

Blue skies smiling at me

Nothing but blue skies do I see.'

'Put a sock in it,' someone yells.

'Well blue's definitely the 'in' colour!' shouts Marguerite. 'The women in my ward are much smarter than those with the red floral numbers.'

'Funny, that,' muses Alison, 'I've seen lots of women in blue, too.'

'Did you notice that the lining of the UNHCR tents is blue?' says Anne, smiling.

'*Was* blue!'

'And very pretty they look, too, gutsy blighters,' puts in Alison. 'Well, okay. My turn!'

We all smile, except the doctor, who is bouncing along in the corner, attempting to read The Lancet.

Alison lifts her chin. 'I actually extracted a tooth all by myself and I've never been so scared in my whole life.'

'No!'

'Yes. There I was, behind the bamboo screen smoking a cigarette to try and stop my hands from shaking, and there he was, poor guy. The only chair I could find in the whole camp was a little straight-backed wooden one, so he had to sit bolt upright. He was holding onto the kidney dish and his hands were shaking even more than mine! The poor guy was terrified! Why on earth there isn't any money for dentists in the camps is beyond me.'

'Go on.'

'I was smoking as hard as I could; had *Where There is no Dentist* on my lap. It said, "Insert the needle until it hits the jawbone, and then squirt." Lordy! I had a pair of pliers and I didn't think I'd be able to do it because I'd pull the guy and his chair right across the *toocle*[5] and out through the bamboo wall. But I had to! The poor guy had toothache so bad. His face was all swollen up and swathed in a scarf.'

'And?'

'I did it! And this afternoon ten more turned up and I pulled out ten more teeth.' Alison leans back proudly. 'Look out! Here comes the tooth fairy!'

Anne giggles. 'You dare touch my teeth and I'll pop a camel spider on your bed.'

'No way!' says Marguerite. 'Talking of spiders is out. I need my beauty sleep. If Alison screams once more when a camel spider drops on her bed, I'll throttle her.'

'Well how would you like it if a spider the size of a dinner plate dropped on you?' retorts Alison.

'Anyway, do you want to hear my stories?' chimes in Marguerite. 'The boys made fifty pairs of sandals from rubber tyres today—that makes seven hundred—all ready for their trek back into Tigray.'

'So they're really going to walk all the way home? What about the arsenic the Derg put in their village wells?'

'They're going. They'll dig more wells, they say. They've got to get back to put seeds in for the next crop.' She bites her lip. 'I've never known such courage ... '

There's a catch in Marguerite's voice as it trails off.

She looks at the others and flushes. ' ... Sorry ... '

Anne reaches over and squeezes her hand. 'Don't be sorry,' she says,

---

5   Toocle: A small round grass hut.

quietly now. 'We've all been … they're the most incredible … '

'Yes they are,' Marguerite says, her voice barely a whisper now.

We all gaze out at the endless sand. Way over in the distance is a camel train, and in between is dry, white sand. A no man's land.

Finally Marguerite turns to look at everyone. 'They are the most amazing people I've ever met.'

We nod.

'How do they keep it up? They're kind. They laugh. They keep lifting themselves up out of the hell … again and again and again …

We are silent. Ahead, Heshe's black curls bounce as he deftly steers the troopie around a stretch of corrugations.

Marguerite pauses. Now a smile flickers. 'Guess where all the wooden lavatory seats went?'

We shrug.

'They turned them into musical instruments—into *krars*. Music everywhere today! Much better for health to have music, and to squat at the loo.' Her laughter is soft. 'Probably not a single person has sat on a toilet seat the whole time we've been here. Why would you? People were dancing to the music.'

'Oh is that where they came from.' Anne chuckles. 'Our pied piper for the TB ward brought in four *krars* for our singing session. It made such a difference. They'd been lying listless for hours and all you could hear was coughing.'

'Look! We're nearly at the Aussie camp,' interrupts Alison. 'I wonder how the bread'll be today? Funny you've never had weevils in yours, Liz.' She glances mischievously at Anne, who winks.

I look up surprised. 'No. I've never had any weevils.'

I look around at the faces. 'Oh no! You've been watching me for the last three weeks!'

They're laughing merrily. 'What did you think we were picking out of our bread? All those black things?'

'But I thought weevils were white?' I say.

THE PRIZE

In 1985 the Shegareb Refugee Camp for 21,000 people was sprawled across the sands near the Ethiopian-Sudanese border. International Aid workers who worked in the camp lived in compounds a half hour drive away across the desert.

The German compound had concrete houses, windows with fly-wire, electric light, air-conditioning, a stone wall, and refrigerators crammed with beer, mettwurst, chocolate, fresh bread, fruit and vegetables.

The Australian compound had straw *toocles* to sleep in, kerosene lanterns, a straw garden wall, camel spiders, old bread with weevils, illegal *aragi* and tinned sardines.

The Irish compound had mud huts, mud walls, solar lights, warm beer and music.

The Tigrayan Refugee Camp had tents, a weekly vitamin C pill, a monthly vitamin A pill, a daily portion of flour, water and, rarely, coal.

The Sudanese had hot wind on desert sands, and camels.

Who do you think dismantled and stole the German generator in the dark of night?

And who do you think laughed?

CAMBODIA

BURNOUT

Shauna dragged herself into her hotel room, bolted the door and sat down on the bed.

So hot. So tired.

It was too much: this morning's pall of smoke over the town as the jungle burnt, land mine explosions in the heat, the silent ward; the silent despair.

The sweet face of that teenager, Bot. He'd been doing so well. And now ... ?

To hell with it.

She looked around. No window, the stench from the toilet in the floor. She hated it. And she hated herself for hating it—she was able to leave, for God's sake! Next week she'd be back in Phnom Penh. With her little Andy.

Stripped to bra and knickers she lay down and stared at the wall. Patterns formed in the brown stains: a water buffalo, a straw house on stilts ...

Was even her subconscious seeing Cambodian images instead of Australian?

She closed her eyes. Ah. She could almost see the blue sky over Manly Beach, feel the cold of the ocean. She could almost hear her little boy's laughter as he learnt to swim.

Thirty minutes. That's all she had before Mony, her translator, was picking her up again in the Toyota. In her mind's eye, she donned a spotted bikini, ran to the ocean edge, and dived in.

The evening sang around the restaurant gazebo where Shauna sat with Mony and three lovely young Kmer waitresses. The air was warm and soft with the fragrance of lemongrass. Shauna gazed out over the fields, conscious of the smoke wafting through the thatch.

How quickly night descended. Fairy lights twinkled and it was hard to discern the man leading his water buffalo home. Across the heavy teak table Shauna watched the young girls laughing with Mony as he chatted to them in Khmer. He was sharing his food, and they giggled and smiled.

At last Mony turned to Shauna. 'They nice girls,' he said as he languidly helped himself to fish. 'Lonely. Far from village. Boss give only small money. Ten dollars every month. How to live? How to send home to family? So I make happy. Give food.' He burst into a torrent of karaoke song. Laughing, he said 'We Khmer love to sing—all the time karaoke!'

He pointed to the sloe-eyed beauty on his right. 'That one—seven brother and sister on rice farm. Farm very small. Father send her this place. Make money to send family. But no money.' He paused, glanced at Shauna's face, and, like a chameleon, whipped a polite smile over his eagerness. 'You okay?'

Shauna quickly straightened in her chair and nodded.

There was an anxious flash in the girls' eyes. They smiled tentatively.

Shauna returned a tired smile across the table to the girls and turned to Mony. 'We need to talk about funding, Mony. I'm sorry, but could we do it now?'

The girls, adept with nuance, swiftly stood up and left.

Friday dawned hot, a crimson sun burning through the smoke haze. In the ward by seven, Shauna had already breakfasted on soup and rice; already she'd heard three explosions; already Mony had nonchalantly said 'landmine' three times.

In the ward there was a sweet smell of blood, sweat and charcoal cooking-fires. Large insects crawled up the walls. Today there were only eight patients lying in the semi-dark, plus numerous family members who squatted on the wooden slat-beds in bare feet. They adjusted saline drips; fed their loved ones from their little cooking pots; nursed babies.

As Shauna walked between patients, a young boy of thirteen or so smiled shyly up at her. He'd lost his foot the previous week. 'Hello,' she said gently, hands brought up in greeting. 'How are you?' He didn't understand, but his smile broadened as he pointed to a pair of wooden crutches nearby.

'Ah! The boys have made you crutches already? You're moving around? Wonderful!' Shauna gave him a warm look and gently took the bandaged foot-stump in both her hands. 'You're doing well,' she said, smiling down at him.

She turned, looking for Mony. He was leaning against the wall, chatting to an old man.

'Where's Chey? Mony! Where's Chey?'

Mony strolled in, smoking a cigarette. 'He come later,' he drawled. 'Maybe lazy.'

'Lazy, eh?' Shauna raised an eyebrow. 'You mean he's consulting somewhere else?'

Mony wouldn't look at her. 'Money for hospital work no enough to feed family.' He laughed, shamed by her directness.

'But how,' Shauna started ... and stopped. Her gaze snapped to the corner.

Bot?

Bot was thrashing about, his face a dark purple, the colour of agony. A red and white checked bandana was clenched between his teeth. He was biting on it so hard it made sharp squeaks. Twenty pairs of eyes turned. The boy's mother was trying to wipe his forehead with a damp cloth, but he kept dashing it away as he writhed.

Shauna moved closer. The mother's gaze flew to her. Tears she couldn't control streaked her face. Shauna looked helplessly back, and then at the young nurse who knelt on the floor beside a metal bucket of frothing, yellow disinfectant. Into it she was dipping the torn meat: the remains of the boy's leg. A small crowd had gathered.

Shocked, Shauna looked for Mony. He'd turned away and was chatting with Sopheap by the door. 'Mony! Where's his pain relief?' Her voice sounded loud in the hushed room.

'What, sister?' Mony's face was impassive.

'I said, where's the boy's pain relief? He must not have the wound cleaned without pain relief!' She was shouting.

Silence. All eyes were on her. Mony took her by the arm and walked her out of the ward. 'They have pain relief, they have pain relief,' he placated, smiling at her.

Angry tears pricked. 'Absolutely. And why ... '

A flicker of nervousness came and went in Mony's eyes. 'You stay here, sister, I go talk with Sopheap.' He smiled again, a smile that didn't reach his eyes. 'We fix it. It okay. It okay.' He hurried away.

Outside now, Shauna realized she was trembling, and recalcitrant tears were threatening a downpour. Smoke from the jungle fires was drifting through the quadrangle and as she gazed out everything seemed to be shimmering.

Steadying herself on the windowsill she summoned the courage to glance back into the dark ward again. The young nurse had stopped the cleaning. She looked confused. The boy lay in a limp heap on the wooden slats, at last allowing his mother's soft touch on his forehead. Over the side of the bed the remains of his leg dangled: grey and yellow shreds. Yellow liquid and blood dripped into the bucket underneath. Stony gazes turned to Shauna.

Soon Sopheap and Mony hurried back, nervous smiles on their faces. 'Boy get injection now,' they asserted as they steered Shauna like an invalid into a tiny office.

In the office, Mony caught Sopheap's eye. The two sat down facing Shauna. Mony took a deep breath. 'Shauna, I tell you story. Here in jungle, Khmer fight many years. We only medics but we make amputations—no proper learn,' he laughed. 'We, village university! We do many, many amputations—sometimes no anaesthetic. Hide in forest. We live like this. Must show courage with pain. Make man strong.'

Shauna was silent, trying desperately to compose herself. 'ATF gave funding for pain relief. Where is it?'

Mony swallowed. 'This place not easy for us.' He hesitated. 'Money given in Phnom Penh, not come to here. It lost somewhere.'

'Okay Mony. You're telling me not to meddle, right?'

'People get kill.'

'But you know the research,' she said, her voice rising. 'If he doesn't have enough pain relief now, he may have chronic pain for years.' She stopped. A toothless old woman was peering in through the office window. 'Oh hell!'

'We fix this,' Mony interrupted, standing up. 'We drive you back to hotel now. You tired. Maybe surprise make you happy?' He winked.

The two men hurriedly left the room. Shauna slowly stood up, picked up her satchel and slung it over her shoulder. 'How can I possibly ... ?' she muttered to the empty room as she wandered, lost, out to the car.

The heat was already frying the town. Exhausted, Shauna stumbled into the darkened hotel foyer. In a corner, a woman in red sat fanning herself. Shauna stopped dead.

'Annie?'

The woman jumped up. 'Thought you might be getting lonely.'

'What on earth are you doing here?'

'I already told you.' She laughed merrily.

'Lord save us! You've come all the way to Cambodia?' Shauna turned to the doorway. 'Mony! Did you know about this?'

He grinned. 'Maybe little bit.'

'What? My sister comes all the way from Australia to Cambodia, then makes her way right out here—God knows how—and you don't tell me?'

Now Annie jumped in. 'Don't, Shauna,' she said in her singsong voice, 'it was my idea. I knew if I told you, you wouldn't let me come.'

'Of course I wouldn't. You're quite mad!'

'Not mad. Just in need of a sisterly hug and a decent shower.'

Shauna opened her arms. She could smell her sister's perfume, the expensive shampoo, saw the flash of red fingernails and gold jewellery. 'Oh, Annie. Come in. I'll make you a coffee—of sorts. Oh, my goodness!' She grabbed Annie's hand, leaving a smiling Mony draped over the front desk, where a pretty receptionist sat.

The two women sat on the bed under the air-conditioning; it was working at last. 'Now tell me what this is really about,' Shauna said firmly.

'I've come to take you and Andy home.'

'What?'

'Shauna, Jake got married last week.'

Silence filled the bedroom. Finally Shauna looked up. 'To her?'

'Yes. To Jenny.'

Outside in the glaring dust, children shrieked. There was the steady thrum of motorbikes, the sharp squeaking of horns. Shauna schooled herself. 'I suppose they looked the picture of joy?'

Annie shrugged. 'Bloss, I'm so sorry. That's why I'm here.'

Shauna stared out at the white heat through the open door. 'You'll need a room,' she said.

That evening Mony drove them to the restaurant. It was a soft, black night. A gecko called like a child, crickets chirped and in the corner of the yard two old men squatted together, talking in gentle voices. The sisters sat under the thatch, drinking beer.

Annie leaned across the table, her face anxious. 'Are you surprised?'

'I shouldn't be, should I? But I am. He didn't let me know. How am I going to tell Andy? Do you know that Jake hasn't sent his son a single letter? Not one!' She played with her glass. 'Did you see my little boy in Phnom Penh?'

Annie reached out to take her hand. 'Yes, I saw him chattering away in Khmer, that sandy hair of his all like a broom. God, Shauna, you left him there.'

Shauna removed her hand, grasped her glass. 'Don't you start giving me a guilt-trip. And don't raise an eyebrow either! He's really happy with Supin and her family.'

'Mmmm?' responded Annie. 'And what about school?'

'Annie! Stop it! He goes to a fabulous international school—and it's not as if I'm away all that often on field trips.' She hesitated. 'When was the wedding?'

'Last Thursday. They're moving to Canberra. Good riddance to bad rubbish. They deserve each other. Jenny's a twit and he's a complete … ' Annie studied her fingernails.

'So you knew?'

'Of course we knew.' Annie shrugged. 'So maybe you can come home now? Andy can meet his cousins—oh Shauna, I'd love that. You so deserve to be happy again.'

Shauna's face softened. She was silent for a while. 'But I'm happy here,' she said hesitantly. 'These people, they … '

At that moment a bee-bopping Khmer tune floated out of her backpack. She gave a wry smile. 'My phone … oh, speak of the devil. Andy!'

'Hi, my most gorgeous little man! How are you going? You're good? Oh, I'm glad. When am I coming home? Not long now—only four more sleeps. You've got a pet lizard called Jesus? Wow! Why don't you like Brent anymore? Well, I think that's fair enough that you don't like him so much after that … oh? Goodnight to you, too, my precious one. You have a good sleep … love you … bye.'

Shauna hung up and shrugged. 'What can I say?'

Annie smiled.

Shauna looked away. 'Shall we call it a day? I'll call Mony. And, Annie … thanks.'

The sisters were in the market early next morning. It was set back from the village main street, next to the hospital. They wandered past wooden stalls selling water pots, bundles of chillies, hessian sacks of rice, hoes. It wasn't very busy as they wandered down the dusty alleyway.

Annie, in a full, lime-green Indian skirt that flashed mirrors, was having a whale of a time. Shauna couldn't help smiling.

'Pineapples how much?' Annie was shouting. She always shouted her English in 'foreign' countries. The wizened stallholder laughed and rattled something off in Khmer.

'What's he saying, Bloss?'

'I don't know. I show how much with my fingers.' Shauna looked sheepish.

'You're kidding! You've been here a whole year and you can't speak Khmer? And even your son's chattering away!' Annie teased as she dived into her handbag to produce a phrase book. 'This is so fun!' Already she had more parcels than she could carry—limes, grapefruit, candles … The little crowd was roaring with laughter as she held up chopsticks and tried to mime a knife and fork.

Shauna watched her. All morning she'd been thinking about her failed marriage, that other life. But now, as she glanced down the market lane, she could hear the soft everyday sounds of the village—the pigs, the motorbikes, the temple bells. She paused. Did she really wish she were back in that marriage? Truthfully?

Her mind drifted to all the families that she visited with Mony—the mothers, the gorgeous children, their clear-eyed balance. She thought of the cow bank they'd started; the pride of those quiet people who now had a cow to care for; a simple prosthesis to enable them to work in the fields. They'd been given back their dignity, hadn't they?

'Hey Annie,' she called, 'feel like a cup of tea?'

Annie turned, gathered up her parcels and moved out of the shade into the sun. 'My goodness, is it hot or is it hot?' She tripped along between the potholes and then stopped.

A scream. Raw. Gravelly. Full throated.

The two women froze. A sudden hush surrounded them. Annie clutched her sister's arm. 'What was that?'

Shauna hesitated. 'That? Oh … nothing.'

The crowd didn't follow them into the teahouse. There was a strained silence in the wooden, open-fronted room. The two sat down and waited for their tea.

'What was that out there?' Annie demanded.

'Alright,' Shauna whispered. 'I think it was a young boy, Bot. No pain relief again.'

'And?'

'He came up from the south. His family is too poor—God, Annie!

They're all too poor!' Now Shauna grabbed a wad of toilet paper from the roll on the table as tears streamed down her face. 'So they sent him here. They're able to clear the jungle and claim the land here, but only the very poor do it because the jungle is infested with land mines.'

'Go on.' Annie was staring intently at her sister's face.

'Bot had only been working a month when he was blown up. I was here when he was brought in. I'm sorry, Annie, I just can't … '

Annie quietly placed her hand over Shauna's.

'It's okay,' Shauna gasped. 'It happens to me every now and then. Sometimes I just can't … ' She laughed weakly and blew her nose forcefully into the toilet paper. 'I fell in love with that kid.' Her voice broke. 'His spunky smile just melts you. Over a week the medics got him walking with crutches. His mother finally arrived—God knows what she used for money to get here. We were about to fit him with an interim prosthesis when his stump got infected and they had to open it again with surgery. And do you know why? He hadn't had enough to eat.'

'Oh.'

'The medics were trying to feed him out of their own funds—they're nice boys—fabulous in fact, but they couldn't afford it. I didn't know he didn't have food. Mony only told me yesterday. He's not to blame.'

'Oh Shauna, it's not your fault, all this.'

'But I raised Bot's hopes! Now look at him. Hear him! Annie, his family … how can they survive if they've got a disabled kid?'

Annie's face was gentle. 'They can, if the project supports them to earn a living. ATF has helped hundreds, haven't they? With their self-help groups and microcredit schemes, the frog and mushroom farms, the cow banks, the training in motorbike repair?'

116

But Shauna's shoulders sagged. 'We can't get enough funding. Land mine victims are no longer 'in' since Princess Diana. I can't make enough difference, Annie! I'm snapping at everyone! I … I keep getting teary. It's not done to cry here.'

Annie handed her another wad of toilet paper. 'Twaddle,' she murmured. She was silent for a while, sipping tea, watching an old woman straighten a little line of cigarettes on a piece of hessian across the road. Finally, she looked directly into her sister's eyes. 'I'm sorry to say this, Shonnoh, but there's a name for the sort of nightmare you're having— and it's no good trying to hide it. It's called burnout.'

Shauna was sobbing uncontrollably, oblivious to the waiters' disdain.

Outside, a man manoeuvred a bicycle through the potholes and dust. Seated behind was a woman nursing a baby whose vein was being fed by a drip held aloft on a bamboo pole. She turned, caught their eyes, and smiled.

A Peacock's Dance

Torben wipes a trickle of perspiration from his face, readjusting his legs on the Kmer-style bench. 'So hot,' he mutters, looking longingly at the fan lying idle in the middle of the room. 'Oh for a Norwegian winter!' He looks out as small clouds of dust blow in from the street.

His blue eyes indulgent, he turns to me. 'I think we must remove Jan soon or we will have some trouble here.'

Sixteen-year-old Jan, his red baseball cap perched backwards on his head, spiked fair hair protruding, is outrageously testing the flirtation threshold of his host.

What a brat!

I want to yell at him, but I say nothing. I'm Torben's guest and Jan is his responsibility, not mine. And it seems Torben knows that our host will do nothing, say nothing.

We watch as three of Mr Yang's daughters shyly gather around the youth on the other wooden sitting platform, overlooking the glare of the street. They're eating mango, delicately, in small pieces from a plate. The boy is singing Norwegian songs, whooping, leaping into dance, everything a peacock might do to attract his hen. I can see that it's the fifteen year-old daughter he's attempting to deflower—the sweet girl with an innocent smile and a shyness that would only draw a peacock closer. Her black hair is held back softly in a coil, loose tendrils framing a round face, the colour of milk coffee. She's too young to use her lustrous hair for seduction, too young to use the dark lashes, the smiles. Instead she wears her feelings for all to see—fear, excitement, innocence. All these for a father to watch, a father whose tongue is stilled by those who hold the keys to his family's future.

Can a young girl be deflowered without the sexual act, without so much as a kiss? Can she be seduced in front of her family and a bunch of foreigners? Am I seeing the girl's sarong and T-shirt being stripped away metaphorically as she bares her heart and is ravished in this simple wooden home?

For there's nothing subtle in our sixteen year old peacock. This is not his first sexual conquest—oh no, he's already bragged to us about his schoolboy exploits, although we can see that his mother's milk still clings to his lips.

Torben stands. 'We must move on,' he says kindly to his host, still with that amusement. There's no apology here for his liberal Scandinavian morality in such a Kmer home, where daughters marry by arrangement, and romantic love is stamped out before it even seeds. Torben nods to the driver who leaps up from the tiled floor to move the luggage out, to open the Land-cruiser doors, polish car seats.

'You have been most kind,' Torben says warmly, clasping Mr Yang's hand in two of his own. 'Your hospitality has been more than generous. Please thank your wife—she is in the kitchen, I presume?'

The man nods, his face unreadable, smile bland. 'It was our pleasure. We will be very happy to accept your training in the hospital.'

I see his gaze slide away from Torben's face as he watches a motorbike bump through the potholes in front of his house.

Mr Yang turns to me. Standing, I bring my hands together in *Namaste*, relieved that we're going. 'Thank you.'

119

Finally, Jan stops guffawing and the girl stops giggling. A bolt of fear flashes over her gentle face as the boy stands, stretches and yawns, all studied nonchalance. He bends over and kisses the girl's cheek, an indifferent gesture. 'See you around,' he drawls as he strolls to the car, climbs in and slams the door, not turning back to see her blush, her anguish.

The family stand formally in a row, fixed smiles on faces as we drive off. We wave and turn away to a future they can never share.

The road is rough. Dodging bikes and chickens, we bounce and jig on the hot back seat, trying to disregard the trickles of sweat down our legs. On either side stretches a mosaic of emerald rice fields, dotted here and there by bamboo huts on stilts, an innocent façade that can easily seduce the mind into a sense of safety, away from the mines that lie hidden in the soil.

A cough brings our attention back to the cloying heat inside the car. Our other passenger sits hunched and small in the corner, silent and withdrawn. Are the feathers of our little peacock drooping?

Torben grins. 'So,' he teases gently. 'How is our Valentino now?'

Jan doesn't look up, but continues to stare out of the window.

'I think I love her,' he whispers truthfully, forlornly.

And I want to hug him. I want to hug all that is naive in our complex world.

THAILAND

THE OLD JESUIT

I hear that music again. So many years afterwards.

Immediately it takes me back to another room, a tiny chapel in the Jesuit Refugee Service in Bangkok. There were six of us, mostly aid workers. We were squeezed into the space for a simple service and the duet came from an old recorder in the corner—a single flute accompanying the sweet, clear voice of a choirboy. Exquisite.

I hadn't noticed the old man sitting next to the recorder until the music started after the readings. He was weeping, and I could see that his long, bent figure was wracked with shame that he couldn't stop the tears.

'I am from Belgium,' he whispered into the room. 'Never before have I seen such pain. I have served the church in Belgium all these sixty years, but never ... '

He stopped, gasping for breath. The music played on, achingly pure.

'They are like animals in the camps! Barbed wire around. Row upon row of huts, all alike and they have lost their legs, their faces, their hope. Where is our God if this terrible thing is happening? What have I done with my life if I haven't been helping? What can I do?'

'Tell your people, Father,' the young priest said quietly. 'Tell them what you have seen, tell them that last week the army towed a barge of refugees into the open sea and sank it. Tell them they are training Kmer Rouge inside the camps. Tell them that the people despair to be sent back to Cambodia.'

'But I am old. If this is the world, then I am broken.'

The music lingered while we shared his grief, our eyes closed tight. In silence we prayed, six ordinary people, each praying to our own version of God.

The old man lifted his head from prayer. He was frail and could not meet our eyes.

UNFINISHED

He has a very erect spine for a Thai monk. On the shoulder that's bare of saffron robe he sports a tattoo.

Presenting himself to me at the beginning of the village temple ceremony, he orders imperiously, 'You take photo. Come!' I feel myself bristling as he leads me into the crowded temple.

I have no idea why I have to take photos. Barely hiding my animosity, I obey. I'm Ajahn's guest after all and there may be loss of face if I refuse this monk who lives with him. Inside, I'm squirming with embarrassment as he marches me from place to place, weaving in and out of village men and women, seated quietly and respectfully on the floor. 'You take photo there! Take that one—that one!' he says in a voice that seems too loud as the ceremony progresses. He points to the presentation of robes, to the rows of monks, the money trees, the gifts of cushions, rakes, brooms, bottled water and rubber thongs. 'You go front now!' he booms, pushing me forward when the 'super monk' addresses us from his high bamboo throne. 'You photo those one!' he says, steering me across the temple floor to photograph the blessing of the Thai 'patrons' from USA.

At last he sits me down (front row and still talking) to photograph the tiny village children dressed in their glittering blue tutus, their lips painted in crimson lipstick, and the lithe school girls doing their traditional dances.

As soon as I can, I escape. I've had enough of being his trophy.

The festival concludes with a bang of fireworks; the crowd performs their last ritual of connecting white cord from one villager to another, right around the hall. The huge rainbow silk balloon is set alight at its rim and, filled with smoke, whooshes into the sky to start its 500 kilometre journey.

The monk returns as I sit peacefully drinking green tea at a cane table under a tree. It's quiet. The heat of the day softens a little as a breeze blows in from the rice fields, bringing a faint scent of cow dung. He turns to me and in that same commanding tone, says,

'You send letter my son. He, Sydney. Two hours.'

I'm not sure what he means and wait to hear more. He turns, marches inside to return with a Maxwell House coffee jar. He makes himself a coffee. I watch as a thin kitten slinks under my chair.

He fiddles with a little camera, finally placing it on the table for me to pick up. A woman cannot take an object straight from a monk's hand. There's a video playing on the tiny screen.

'My daughter. She work Unilever Bangkok. This picture Unilever work.'

A young girl with lush black hair, a rose-pink blouse and black skirt sits at a little computer station in an empty office. We see the huge room and her photo pinned on a board behind her workstation. We see her pretending to type, we see the photocopier and how she pretends to make a copy of a letter. She is standing in a huge, silent room. The room gleams white and chrome with its scores of empty computer stations in front of long, empty benches. I guess it's a holiday.

The video seems to go on forever, showing the same thing over and over, and twice I pass it back, but each time he pushes it back across the table to me, pointing out her desk, the doorway and the photocopier.

How many times has he watched this?

'My son. Marry girl Philippines. Two child. He work restaurant, Australia. Not find. Green card.'

He is talking about his son.

'Do you know where he is?' I ask.

'No. Not know."

'Can you email him?'

'No email.'

Still I don't understand what he wants of me. To find him? I give him my email address to send to his daughter. 'But I live far away from Sydney,' I say. Has the son left the family with another woman? Has she left? Is he hiding without a visa? And the monk. Why? Was poverty the driving force for him to enter a monastery?

'Your daughter—she looks for her brother?' I ask.

'Yes. No find. You find!'

I point to my email address on the scrap of paper in front of him. 'Send this to your daughter. By post. That is the best way. She can talk with me.'

I look across at him. He sits looking at the folded piece of paper with the email address, beside his mug of coffee. His head is hanging from the ramrod-straight spine like a broken puppet. Slowly he reaches out and picks up the paper, holding it like a lotus between two hands, two old hands. He looks up and shame trembles in his eyes.

He can't read? I realise that I want to hug him fiercely, hug away his hurt, his longing, his helpless loneliness. But a woman mustn't touch a monk. 'Send it to your daughter,' I say.

Behind us, on the half-constructed pagoda, prayer flags flutter. Children scream in delight from the heights of a pile of sand.

Next day I leave the village.

I don't see the monk again. The daughter never contacts me. I never find out what happened.

He's still there, though: an itch under my skin. I could have done more. Why didn't I?

FRIED HABITUALLY DRUNK

In Thailand recently I was intrigued to find a choice on a restaurant menu between Fried Habitually Drunk with Shrimps, and Fried Habitually Drunk with Chicken. Given there were also Grilled Snake's Head and Baked Silkworms I chose the drunk chicken and, other than wondering how much alcohol the poor village fowl had needed to be habitually drunk, thought no more about it. That is, until I returned home to Australia. Then I realized that it was me who was fried habitually drunk.

The problem is this: to live in Australia these days is a befuddlement.

It starts even before your plane touches down on Australian soil. You look up from your seat by the window, and there is a leering flight attendant spraying you with poison. It could be our government's way of keeping the numbers down, I suppose, like putting refugees onto tiny islands surrounded by lots of ocean.

After the delousing you're herded off the plane into a hall called 'Goods to Declare'.

'What soil did your feet touch in the last four weeks?' asks an officious woman, the shape of a wardrobe.

'Pretty muddy actually—the monsoon you know—but some parts were sandy.'

'Show me your shoes!' she barks.

'Well, there came a point where I just had to throw them away.'

The woman's eyes narrow. 'And what is this?' she hisses as she extracts a little red box from my backpack.

Oh no! My green bean cakes. Wardrobe opens the little packet to reveal what looks like a cow turd. 'This must be confiscated.' She's gleeful. I think maybe in her next life she'll graduate to a parking inspector.

'And now the cushion. Under your arm. Give it to me. We'll burn it. Heil Hitler.' Her face glows with pleasure.

I jam the cushion into my armpit. She can amputate my arm if she wishes—and she probably does wish, but she isn't getting my cushion. 'This was given to me,' I say firmly. 'A real privilege.'

'It'll cost you $60 for fumigation.' She puts her hands on her hips. Smile of an anaconda.

'$60! No! It's a gift from a monk.'

She sneers. Oh may she become a hungry ghost in her next life. But if she burns my cushion will my next lifetime be as a mangy dog in Calcutta?

The counter dividing us, Wardrobe looks disdainfully at my lowliness. I'm betting that if I give it to her she'll stick it up her jumper and take it home. It'd be easy; her breasts are that rectangular shape anyway.

I try one last rear-guard action. 'Could I unpick it and let all the stuffing out?' I smile at her.

To my astonishment she suddenly agrees, grabs the offending article with its little purple and pink stripes, slashes it viciously at both ends with a knife and marches me over to a huge bin.

'I'll do it if you are busy,' I venture. Careful now or she'll throw it at me. But no! There's a distraction. Three whacking big attacker dogs are careering around and around the hall with wads of towelling in their jaws, and little men in uniform yelling Good Dog! Good Dog! It's pandemonium.

Wardrobe won't let me touch my cushion now as, with pernickety care, her hands in white cotton gloves, she extracts a bin full of kapok from its six compartments.

Fourteen minutes go by. I am counting because I have a connecting plane to catch and I'm going to miss it. I suspect she knows this.

'Goodness!' I say after a while. 'That's a lot of kapok.'

Kapok is floating in little nose-tickling strands across the hall and Wardrobe is beginning to look like my drunk chickens, except her feathers are white, and those Thai chickens are invariably black.

At last she's finished and I smile.

'You are worth your weight in gold,' I say as I hasten away towards freedom. That is one hell of a lot of gold.

She turns her back on me, walks behind the counter and unsheathes her claws. Her next victim, a little old lady, is standing cowering on the mean side of the counter, holding a goldfish in a plastic bag.

I manage to catch my connecting flight with my sad cushion tucked in a book like a burst balloon. And then more habitually drunken things start to happen: my cell phone dies. I'm pretty sad about this. Over three years, my daughter patiently taught me how to drive it and I'd been able to ring home from the supermarket and ask how many long-life milks we had left in the pantry.

Needing a new phone, I find the address of a telephone shop in the pink pages. And that's another story: how can anyone find anything in all those phone books? Is a mobile phone pink pages? Yellow? Or white? Local government or Commonwealth? Maybe if it's tapped, it's Commonwealth?

Eventually I find a telephone shop. A fresh-faced young man looks up from his computer and smiles a lovely welcome.

'Your name?'

'Liz.'

'Your password?'

Password? Oh my Lord. I can't remember things like that, but I have it in my handbag. Oh blast! I've left my handbag at home having used a body belt for the last three months on account of preferring not to be murdered.

'Birth date of your mother?'

'Good Lord.'

'Existing phone plan?'

'I planned to find out what time my daughter might be home for tea.'

The dear boy stares into a computer, typing all sorts of numbers, codes and odd foreign words. I stare at the back of the computer screen, wondering if I should ring Centrelink to tell them I'll be late, except I can't, because I need a phone and in order to have a phone I have to know my mother's birth-date. I sit down.

He picks up another phone. 'Oh Hi, I'm Vic from SA, password 'gooseberry'. I have a customer here, wants a *flug slosh* and is converting to a *snig eblim*, but she will need a BMX, won't she?'

He turns to me. 'Do you have BMX?'

'No. I wish … ' I close my eyes. I am in for the long haul. Breathe in and smile; breathe out and smile.

He looks at me with a very strained smile of his own. 'You were on an *ishy slosh* plan and I suggest you go on a *plidge*. It'll only cost you $30 for six months instead of $20 each month. Of course, direct debiting would be in your favour as against prepaid. And you'll need a new phone rather than a *bling*. It's on special, reduced to $139. A real bargain, eh?'

Ah!

'Okay,' I say, standing up. A bargain? Far be it for me to question. I might get a bling instead of a wop and then I'll be in real trouble. I reach for my credit card. One hundred and thirty nine dollars. I understand those words anyway.

'Of course the plan of free calls for ten minutes between six and seven won't apply but ... '

'I'll take it,' I say. 'I have to be somewhere else so can I get it and run?'

'Do you have your driver's licence? I need identification.'

'No. I left my handbag ... '

The young thing looks up. 'I can't do it without identification,' he says firmly. 'Do come in again some time.'

I rush to Centrelink, wait in a long line of ordinary people like me. Finally, I reach the counter. 'I'd like to get support for my phone bill. It says here on this form ... '

The man looks at me with benevolence. 'Dearie, you go down to the department of Youth and Social Services. They are the very people.'

I cruise around the streets in my car—that's another story: where do you find the oil dipstick? Eventually I find the place and walk in. 'I would like support for my phone bill ... '

The woman is a PNN (Professional: No Nonsense.) 'You're in the wrong place. Centrelink is where you need to be. We only deal with hardship. And not having a phone is not a hardship.'

I'm beginning to think she's right. Not having anything might actually be a luxury. But the treadmill has got me by the short and curlies.

Back at Centrelink I am confronted with another little man. 'Phone support? Just go home, dear, and ring your phone company.'

Ten dollars of petrol later and four dollars fifty for an ice cream to cheer me up, I arrive home and ring the phone company.

'Your call is important to us and has been placed in a queue. It may be monitored for communist purposes. If your enquiry is about who won the election, press one. If it's about who should have won the election, press two. To reduce your phone bill, play Chopin's Revolutionary without a mistake. Do not pass go and do not collect two hundred pounds.'

I'm thinking about a village in Thailand where a monk might be beating the deep, dawn drum and the gentle sound drifts over little wooden houses into people's dreams. The air is soft and warm. The monk looks out over the rice fields as early light caresses the mist. Soon the scent of cooking fires will drift across the yard. A dog stands up and stretches as a cowbell tinkles.

He walks quietly to the wooden temple. Chanting will soon begin.

NO MAN'S LAND

BROWN PAPER PACKAGES
TIED UP WITH STRING

Charles jolts awake. Is it morning? He fumbles with the light switch beside his pillow. 4am. At least two hours until dawn. Four hours to breakfast, six to morning tea and a biscuit, eight to lunch …

His back hurts. His soul hurts. He needs his radio—Radio National. Why won't they set that up for him? Why won't they … ? Why …

He shuts his eyes.

String, he thinks. There's something rather elemental about string—comforting and elemental. String wound around a bundle of old plumbing pipes—like that wine rack he made …

Yes. That's what he is—a bundle of old tubing held together by string. One tube for the nurses to shovel food through, two to stick amplifiers into, one to extract shit from, one to cover with a pad to stop it leaking …

But string. That's nice. Being held together by it. Homely and useful, string. Earthy. Like brown paper … for parcels … being parcelled about … posted … sent … handled …

But had he arrived? Had anyone opened this parcel and found him? Maybe he was in lost property?

He looks up. His door is opening.

'You awake, Charlie love?'

He quickly closes his eyes.

'You didn't have your bowels opened yesterday, did you dear?'

Slowly he opens his eyes again and stares at her. Bowels. The bowels of the earth. Jules Verne. Clever, that author ...

'Charlie! Wakey wakey—your bowels?'

She's coming into focus. It's that one, he thinks, the squarish one with the limp. Pretty hair. Wanting him to do something about one of his tubes ...

Compliant, that's what he is—always was, rather.

He starts to roll over, rocking back and forth. The bedclothes are too tight. Can't sit up ...

'Here, Charlie, let's get you to sitting ... ' the nurse says. Her voice is squeaky. A bit like the linoleum in the corridors. He hates linoleum. He starts to stand up, rocking back and forth to build up momentum. 'I'll go to the bathroom now,' he mutters, his voice thin as a ribbon. He shifts his feet into brown slippers. Nice and warm, slippers ...

'Yeah. That's the boy. Let me give you a hand, sweetheart.'

Give me a hand? He looks at her again. 'But don't untie the string,' he mumbles.

'What's that, Charlie?'

He feels the arm around his waist, pushing; around his fawn woolly dressing gown, the one Gwen gave him. His feet can't keep up with the pushing.

'I'm a wine rack,' he mumbles.

He doesn't know why he wheels his walking frame to the door and peeks out. A sound? He can see the nurse's station from his doorway. The square one is slumped on a pile of folders. She's asleep, he thinks.

139

The sound is louder out here—like a buzzer. A light is flashing over the door of the room next to his, the one with the new lady—Shirley, is it? He looks again at the sleeping nurse and makes a decision; turns his walker and pads towards the new lady's door in his slippers. They make a soft swishing noise.

At her door, he hesitates. Should he have woken the nurse? He tries to lift his hand to the door handle. It goes every which way, the tremor always worse when he is nervous. At last he has a grasp on the handle and can turn it. The door squeaks as it opens and there is only muted light inside the new lady's room. He pushes the walking frame inside. 'Are you okay?' he asks, his voice coming out like a trickle of water.

Obviously not. He can see her hearing aids on the bedside table, the hump of her body curved into the foetal position under the white coverlet. And he can hear her sobbing.

'What can I do?' he asks. 'Is there something?' His reedy voice fades.

Still she's crying. What should he do? The nurse is coming down the passage. It's none of his business. He tries to back out but his body starts shaking. The walker begins to rock. He topples sideways into the door jam.

'Charlie! For crying out loud! What on earth?'

Charles tries to say something but the words are stuck somewhere. His dressing gown has come open and the fly of his pyjamas is gaping. 'Her eye pipes are leaking,' he manages to whisper as he lets himself be led back to his room. 'Badly.'

He doesn't want to come to lunch. The new lady'll be there and she'll think he's a voyeur. The gong went ten minutes ago, but still he's sitting on his bed. He can smell it; he can even smell the crispiness of it. A roast—lamb, mint sauce, roast spuds, carrots, parsnips—maybe two bits? Gravy, peas. He looks at his walker. Could he chance it? Could he just go down to the dining room and tell them he wants his on a tray in his room? He checks himself in the mirror and rubs at the bit of egg that he spilt on his cashmere pullover—Gwen always said he was a messer—and then he turns his walker to the door. Soon he is shuffling down the corridor.

'Ah there you are Charlie!' says the tall one. Maureen, is it? 'I was just about giving up on you!' She grabs his walker and propels him to his seat. 'Your dinner's getting cold. Sit ye down, love—here at the end of the table with Shirley,' she says with a push.

'I want a tray,' he whispers, but the helper has bustled off. He keeps his eyes down as he picks up his knife and fork. Even his plate is embarrassing, with sides on it like those bunny plates for toddlers. He's sure Shirley is looking at it.

The others are shovelling food into their tubes very fast. It's like a race, he thinks. He wonders what the prize is? More custard? If he won, he'd like another parsnip—but hot and browned on the outside. Not like these cold ones. They go squishy when they're cold …

The lady on his left must be bonkers, he reckons. She's cramming in her roast while reciting the Lord's Prayer.

'Ourfatherwhichartinheavenhallowedbethyname … ' He thinks that she'll be the winner today. She's already scraping up the gravy, and he's only just managed to spear the first bit of cold lamb. Lots of food down the mouth tubes, he thinks. What about YouTube?

He looks up. Oh God, the new lady—Shirley—is looking at him. He can feel a blush seeping up his cheeks. His fork shoots across his plate.

'Hello,' he manages.

She smiles just a little bit. It is a nice smile, but wobbly. Awkward. 'Hello,' she replies.

They continue their meal in silence. The others at the table are long gone and only Shirley and Charles remain, both of them eating slowly. It's time for the two fruits and yellow custard.

'At least they don't cajole air down our nose tubes ... ' Charles says, unaware that he has thought out loud.

He sees Shirley pause. She seems to be making up her mind about something, fiddling with her serviette, rolling it up and pushing it through a silver serviette holder. Nice, that holder; she must have brought it from home.

Now she looks up. 'Cajole?' she says at last, her voice wavery, as if she is too scared to ask. 'Did you say cajole, Mr Martin?'

Charles' chewing slows down and stops. He waits while words line up in his head. 'Yeah,' he whispers. 'Cajole, soothe by flattery, persuade ... ' The words rush out in a monotone and stop.

Shirley places the serviette in its holder beside her plate. 'Mr Martin?'

'Yes,' he acknowledges, looking at her at last and steadying the tremor in his hand on the edge of the table.

'Mr Martin,' she says again. He sees a slither of hope lighting her eyes. 'You wouldn't by any chance play scrabble, would you?'

Again he waits for the words. He tugs at his own serviette that the tall one stuffed into his collar. It drops on his lap. 'As a matter-of-fact I do', he says at last, the words rushing out across the room.

He wishes he could smile his gratitude.

They are seated at a little table in the anteroom. A bland seascape stares down from a pale apricot wall behind them. Pale turquoise full-length curtains block out the night. Charles thinks it could be raining and wonders how he could tell. In front of the table the corridor stretches all the way down to the nurse's station.

'There you go, dearies.' It's the night nurse again, fussing. 'You sure you're warm enough, Charlie love?' she asks as she tucks a pink mohair blanket around him.

He nods, feeling that horrible crawl of heat up his cheeks. He wants to run. Knows he can't. Can hardly walk. He watches as the nurse plonks the green bag of letters onto the scrabble board. 'May the best man ... or woman ... win!' she says and her little laugh sounds silly as she heads off at speed down the wide passage.

Shirley gives him a small smile. 'She's not very happy ... in a bit of a state,' she says tentatively.

'The square one?' he asks innocently.

Shirley bursts out laughing. He looks at her. She's nice when she laughs, he thinks. More feisty, somehow, than he originally thought. That was one thing about Gwen. She wasn't all that feisty.

'Yes, the square one,' Shirley goes on, looking embarrassed now. He wonders if it is because she laughed. 'Her name's Susie. A single mum with twin boys.' She looks away towards the curtains, towards the Outside and is quiet for a while. He waits. He can see her pulling herself back to here; the effort it takes. 'They're only fourteen,' she resumes with a polite little smile. 'She leaves them home alone while she's on night duty.' Shirley stops, stoops down to open her handbag. 'What did I bring a handbag for?' Her laugh is brittle now. 'Habit, I suppose.' She looks at him again. 'Sorry. I guess I shouldn't ... I don't know the rules.'

Charles stares at her and tries to shake his head. He waits for the words. 'Don't apologise,' he eventually manages. He would like to reach out and place his hand over hers. He would have done that with Gwen. He looks down at his hand. It reminds him of a well-oiled piston in a ship's engine. Back and forth, back and forth, back and forth, back and forth. Never stopping. Never, ever stopping. He looks down the passage. The nurse—Susie—is speeding down past his room ... rubber-soled shoes ... and suddenly he's remembering last night. What had the nurse thought?

Shirley coughs gently. 'Shall we play?' she asks quietly. She picks up the bag, opens it and offers it to Charles. 'Would you like to pick a letter?' she asks.

He takes a deep breath, uses one hand to steady the other and reaches into the bag. An N. He hands the bag to Shirley. She delves in —an E.

'I'm first,' she says. 'But before we start,' she looks at him hesitantly, 'would you mind awfully if I ask you a personal question? Please say no if you'd rather I didn't ... '

Charles feels a shrinking inside. He nods.

'Were you called Charlie or Charles at home?'

He looks down at the N in his hand, waits for the word to form in his mind. 'Charles,' he whispers. He sees the sound shrinking into the space until it disappears. He can't look at her. Instead he reaches for the bag and grabs a handful of letters, separates seven and pulls them across the board towards him.

Shirley shifts in her chair. 'Would it be okay with you if I call you Charles?' she asks. 'I just don't think Charlie ... the way the nurses ... '
She arranges her seven letters on the wooden holder.

Charles feels tears welling up inside him and tries desperately to quell them. As he nods, the tremor in his hand increases and a letter shoots off the board and lands on the floor. He looks at it, stricken.

'We'll get the tea lady to pick it up,' Shirley says now. A firmness has entered her voice.

He can hear the trolley rumbling along the corridor. He waits, mute, while it moves from door to door. 'Tea or coffee, Bert, love?' 'Tea or coffee, Alice, love?'

At last it reaches their table. 'Please could you pick up that letter from the floor, Jean,' asks Shirley promptly.

Charles sees the quick smirk on the girl's face. He thinks of the safety of his room, the feel of the dressing gown around him.

'Here, love,' the girl is saying to him. 'Let me arrange your letters for you. Look—this biscuit dish'll do ... a nice rectangle, Charlie. It'll make it easier for arranging your letters.' She tips the biscuits onto the trolley, swoops up Charles' letters and arranges them for him on the plate in front of him. He cowers.

At last all the two can hear is the receding sound of the trolley down the passage. Charles stares at the letters. Slowly they come into focus and he sees that the tea lady has already made a word for him, the wrong word.

Shirley is placing letters across the double word line:

She does this with a forefinger and, peering close, she shifts them into position.

145

Ft his? Charles stares and suddenly sees it and a laugh forms somewhere in his toes. It bubbles up his legs and shoots through his throat into one joyful, silent laugh.

Across the table Shirley is beaming. 'It's your turn,' she says.

He reaches for the green bag, grabs a handful of letters and spreads them out.

'Rules are meant to be broken—that's a cliché,' rushes out. Carefully, using two hands, he spreads his word downward.

He draws a shaky question mark on the board below the 'T' with his finger.

Shirley grins, delves into the green bag herself and brings out a fistful of letters, scatters them on the table and makes a word ...

She draws a question mark with her finger after 'N'.

He looks across the table and sees a face full of humour, and hope, and just a tinge of trepidation. A beautiful human face.

She's starting to giggle.

His shoulders start bouncing again with silent laughter. The laughter increases his tremor. At last he picks out two letters ... a 'Y' and an 'S'. He places them appropriately and watches her wonderful free giggling as she reaches for another handful of letters ...

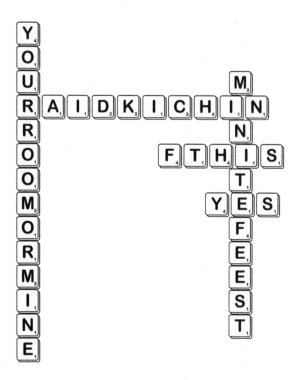

'That's a three-times-triple-word score,' she murmurs.

He looks at the board and his monotone face crinkles and cracks into a very human smile.

Susie is not asleep when Charles shuffles past the nurse's station with his walker carrying a bicycle basket-full of bottles, packets and jars, but she pretends to be. She is not asleep as he heads into Shirley's room. But she pretends to be.

Poor kid, Charles thinks, as he passes her, her head resting on a pile of files. She's got it tough.

I LOVED RED

Them days I loved wearing red. Not that pillar box red. Crimson. But these days, who cares what I wear—who's there to see? I might have on me favourite green striped beanie, purple leggings, orange woolly dress or black oilskins. I like it like that.

But I do draw a line somewhere, like I always dress for bed. In me Methodist nightie, all soft and warm to curl feet into, especially if there's a hottie in that stripy wool cover between the legs.

I suppose I'm noticing the cold more these days—but is it more that I notice these days? Take cold, for instance. The bloody marvel of it. It whips your face when you head out into the channel in the tinny, or it's in that drip that runs down the paddle of your canoe. It's your special cold—watery, salt cold, like on bare feet when you haul the tinny to shore. I love that, because it's the dead opposite of warmth—about as opposite as you could get from woolly socks, a pot-belly and me steamy bath on its wonky legs.

Yes, I notice these days alright—pelicans, black swans, shags—me darlings without even a swear word in their heads. They're like your kids, them birds.

I'm not asking for anything. I've got time now, oodles of it. Or time has me, more like. That Old Man Time—he stretches right out and turns in circles. Even stops. Never races though, not any more, not even when that old wind howls down the Channel, blowing me clean across the jetty onto the railing, just while I'm doing me darnedest with them ropes to tether the tinny fast. But them storms are just doing their thing. Yeah, Time has me round his little finger, eh.

Night-time stretches like chewing gum too. Sometimes I lie awake in me little bed by the window. How long is it since I been in the double one with Artie? Cripes, I can't even remember what Artie felt like. I like to lie and look at the stars. And them stars are like stars should be, just like out of Andamooka where they all fell onto the edge of the gibber. Here I hear them call me, especially them black nights without town lights nowhere to spoil it.

Lately I've been listening to swans. They come a few months back since the Murray mouth silted up. They pipe away like blowing through a bit of bamboo—all musical—up and down, up and down. And then there's the sound of water slapping against the tinny or those mean little waves on the mud shore when the wind's up. In summer them Cape Baron geese honk from the island and the sound is that clear you'd never even think the Channel were in between. And me little shack talks too, sometimes with the scrape of the wattle tree on the tin or just the shack stretching and curling up for a snooze. Jeez I love this place.

A few years back I needed talk back radio for company in the nights, but somehow the watery noises won. Sometimes I wonder why I lie in a bed at all—the earth'd be enough, I reckon. Because that earth is doing a good job of calling me too.

Day-times I wander round the sand dunes and usually I'm that busy I don't notice that Old Man push the sun up and then down again to trick me. I suppose I like chatting as I poke around in me bare feet and thank God there's no human being to listen. I don't need human beings. They don't listen, not like animals do—and the bushes. You know, even insects'll listen to you if they think you're right in the head—and they'll answer you—fair in the stomach. Like me sideways beetle, slipping, starting again, leaving its train line behind. If you listen good, your soul can float right over into that beetle.

Talking of human beings, of course there's Sollo, but I can't really class him as a human being, can I? I supposed he is one. But Sollo is more comfy, like me beetle. Sollo even looks like me beetle. I can see him now from the tinny. He's waving from that pink armchair perched on the end of his jetty—one day that jetty's going to just collapse underneath him.

'Hey, you old bag! If you've got fish, I've got soup!' he's yelling.

'Can't hear you, you fat ol' bastard!' I'm shouting back from the boat, settling meself all comfy now beside the tiller and revving the engine a bit.

'I said ... come and get it!' He's roaring through his hands.

'Come and get what?' I know darned well what he means.

'Anything you like!' he's answering. Still with that maroon scrappy jumper pulled half down over his paunch. Doesn't he ever wear anything else?

I'm turning me head away so he can't see any smiling, then I'm putting the engine into full throttle and shooting off down the channel. I like soup.

Me shack's ten doors down from Sollo's and I'm glad no-one lives in the ones between. I pull the tinny up through the mud onto the salt-water couch—low tides—and grab the bucket of fish. Soon I'm padding in through the open door straight into me kitchen. Nice and warm—a pot belly'll never let a girl down. It doesn't take two shakes to throw on some socks and sneakers, me op-shop coat and beanie and I'm off down the dirt road and into Sollo's through the back door.

'You know … ' I ease meself up on his one and only stool by the bar. 'I was thinking while I was down there in the Coorong … ' I'm giving him one of those sideways looks.

'And?' mutters Sollo without turning from stirring the pot on his wood stove.

'I was thinking that you and that sideways walking beetle have got some similar charicheristicas … '

'And you telling me this before I serve up your soup?' But the bugger doesn't turn, just stands easy, legs apart, toes spread out in his thongs.

'It's just about the biggest compliment a girl could give … '

'A beetle?'

'No. Not just a beetle. My beetle. He's me friend… '

'Well you get that, I expect.' He ladles the soup all hot into two mugs and slides one across the bar to me. 'What you want to do with that fish?'

'If it were me, I'd chuck it in the oven. Them days I'd-a-soaked it in lemon, wrapped it in paper-bark real good and hit the bottle while it cooked on the coals. I tried too hard. Chuck it in as it is. Coorong mullet's pretty happy just plain cooked.'

Sollo's nodding and brings out a tin tray, slaps the fish in a row and slides it all into the oven. 'I'd give it fifteen minutes, wouldn't you?'

'Who's counting?' I'm flicking through his fishing magazine.

He says nothing but is slowly lowering that old body of his into the armchair in the corner with all its springs hanging out. Doesn't spill a drop of soup—but neither is he noticing that spider crawling on the wall right behind his head.

Me and Sollo are sipping for a while, without saying nothing. I'm looking out onto the Channel through his window smeared all with salt. The sea mist's creeping in; you can't even see the island and the swans have gone all quiet. Somewhere between the sea and the sky … no … it must be at the point of where the sea meets the sky, I reckon, but where?

'Orright!' Sollo booms.

I hit the ceiling.

'Orright what?'

'If I'm a beetle, then you're a bloody emu.' He finishes triumphant, legs apart in the armchair and a tea towel tucked into the neck of his jumper.

'But mine was a compliment, I told you … '

'Who says an emu isn't a compliment then?' he roars. He's getting deaf, old Sollo. 'You got emu legs, emu knees. A bit skinny for the middle part, but the rest—you'll do.'

'You taking a rise out-a me, you old bugger? What if I like emu and you telling me is dead on the knocker? Hey that fish'll be done … ' I hop off me stool and poke over to the wood stove, open the door and peer in. 'You got bread?'

'Damper do you?'

'Yeah.'

I pull out the fish, plonking three each onto his tin plates.

For a while I'm thinking just about the eating of me fish. But then the other thought comes back. I turn to Sollo. Careful.

'You know I was looking out there on the Channel,' I say and me mouth's rather full, 'and I was wondering where I should look to see them water spirits. I reckon it's where the sky meets the sea. But the sea's meeting the sky all over the place ... you seen them, Sollo?'

Was that casual enough? This costs pride, this question.

'Seen 'em?' There's a doozie of a pause. 'Yeah, sometimes.' He shifts in his chair.

'So where? You bugger!' I'm a bit snappy.

Sollo fidgets a bit, looking hard at a bit of damper in his hand. 'Yeah, well I seen 'em ... where the oar dips ... ' He's hesitating again, and looks away as if that calendar on the wall is pretty interesting.

'Bloody ripper!' I'm dumping me plate with a whacking clang on the bench and the smiling just about reaches me ears. 'So, when you separate the sky from the sea with your oar, something gets born—like water spirits!'

Sollo's back staring at his damper. 'Could be ... '

'So that means ... ' I'm hopping off me stool and bouncing from one foot to the other—I do that sometimes. 'That afore that, there was no separation, so that's where God's hiding.'

Sollo looks up all startled but I reckon I've got to keep on with this.

'You ever felt like you had no separation from them birds out there, or from the stars, for instance?'

Sollo sits and thinks for a bit, chewing real slow. 'Maybe.'

'So do you reckon that's God?'

Sollo looks away. 'Yeah. Always thought that.'

'Not God up there in the sky?'

Sollo looks real uncomfortable now. 'I don't ... '

There's a knock at the door. Me and Sollo both go dead still, our eyes popping. Real careful, Sollo's putting his plate on the floor and lifts his hand up to warn me. I'm nodding. We're both staring at the door—and jump sky high when the knock comes again, even louder.

Still we don't move, watching shit-scared as the knob turns and the door creaks open. Then this oblong female face with one of them no-nonsense haircuts pokes in.

'Oh, Hi! Excuse me for disturbing you,' she's saying with one of those smiles that looks like a Tiger snake. 'May I come in?'

'Well you in already ain't you?' That's me snapping.

The woman's lips go real thin. She shuts the door behind her and makes her way clip clop on high-heeled shoes across Sollo's wooden floor.

Now me and Sollo pick up our plates and start to mop up our fish juice with bits of damper. You'd think we hadn't eaten since Christmas, we're looking that hard at our plates.

'I came to deliver these,' the woman says, edgy now. She plops two letters on the bar beside me, her red nail polish flashing. 'I'm sorry to inform you of the council's decision, but you will be relocated in the Christian Centre for the Ageing ... '

Still us-two keep mopping, and I'm looking at meself reflected in Sollo's window and seeing me hair escaping in bits and pieces from me beanie and Sollo's tea towel dangling.

The woman licks her lips—they're a puce colour. 'These shacks have been condemned. They are to be bulldozed. You are to be relocated as I said before ... '

The silence that follows is that loud it'd deafen a pelican. Then

'Get out!' Sollo roars.

The woman's off like a rocket.

I'm marching across the sand-hills to the Coorong beach. Wearing that old red taffeta dress and it's hanging a bit now that I've lost me curves. I'm pretty glad I've got me little black billy and I'm swinging it, listening to the lump of damper bouncing around. In the other hand I'm holding onto that photo of me shack for dear life.

Behind me trudges Sollo. He's been looking grey in the face lately. And he's been staggering a bit. Shit. The last weeks've just about wiped out that man. Sodding bastards. Now we've got no home, no bloody prospect of freedom to breathe. And what sort of a circus was that old people's home? Makes me want to throw up to even think about it.

I'm turning to Sollo. 'You know, if one more human being smiled at me I'd sock them fair in the eye. Them people that run that old folk's place was all loony—every one of them!'

Sollo just nods. He's probably still thinking about me tinny going down engine and all after we holed it. 'Them bastards ain't going to get me tinny!' I was screaming pretty hard as we stood there and watched it sink.

'Them bastards ain't going to get me and you, neither,' I'm spitting now. 'C'mon Sollo! The last thing you do is to let them beat you.'

Sollo stops and looks at me. 'Yeah,' he says, and, lifting his head, he plods on.

'You game, Sollo?' I'm shrieking as I prance down the beach towards the roaring surf, me red skirt flapping around in the wind.

'You bet I'm game,' he hollers. 'But there's a bit of a problem. I can't swim.'

'What do you mean, you can't swim?'

'I can't bloody swim!' he shouts.

Well now I'm yelling. 'Well lucky old you! You're only seventy five and you can't swim, and I'm nearing eighty five and I swim that good that I'll reach Kangaroo Island afore I drown. All you have to do is wade out there and snuff it—you gone!' I'm hopping from one foot to the other now, watching Sollo as he's hesitating on the water's edge. Me eyes narrow. 'You not going to chicken out on me now are you?'

'How can I drown if I can't swim out far enough?' he's muttering.

'Oh Lord. I'll have to life-save you by the neck to get you out past the breakers.' But I look at the way he's standing there and me voice goes pretty soft. ''Ere, me mate, me precious beetle, come 'ere. I'll take you out. Don't worry about water. If anything was your friend, water would be … '

Sollo steps over the foam real gingerly to reach me. 'Jeez! It's cold!'

'Nah! It's just making sure you noticing.'

'Yeah, I'm bloody noticing. No bloody home, no boat. Fucking old folk's home. Ah! Stuff it, Nel!'

He grabs me hand and in we go, swearing as we jump each roller, and I'm aware orright of the wild look in Sollo's eyes as the swirling water gets deeper. Neither me nor him is looking too much at them gulls nor the pinky colours of the beach with a lone billy sitting there.

Five minutes later I'm shrieking 'Sollo! Quit it! We're not ready to drown yet! Sollo!'

But Sollo's threshing wildly and me grip around his neck doesn't help one bit.

Now I'm yelling. 'I can't hear myself think. Float, for God's sake! Sollo, stop it! You're pulling me down!'

Our feet hit the bottom with an almighty bump. Sollo's wiping the water out of his eyes, facing the beach, I'm coughing. And then I look up ...

'Oh, shit! Look out!' A wave like Ayers Rock's coming, all power and thunder.

'F u u c c k k !'

I let go of Sollo and us-both are hurled in somersaults. Is this it? It's a bloody panic!

Legs are everywhere as with a whoosh we land on the beach.

'Jesus wept,' I'm muttering and I'm lying face flat on the sand in me sodden red dress. 'That was a mighty big fella ... '

'Yeah.'

I lift me head. 'Look at you, Sollo. You're all spread-eagled like one of them beached whales.'

Sollo's breathing pretty heavy. 'Maybe we should try on the Coorong side where it's dead flat? ... ' He's gasping.

'Nah. I'd just swim to the other side of the Coorong without even getting tired—no hope in hell of drowning. And I'd probably bring you with me.'

Slowly we're sitting up and crawling up the beach. I see Sollo's wearing his boxer underpants and still has that maroon jumper. 'No,

Sollo, you got to think different—like, look at those waves roaring and dumping all over the place—it's just show. It's only water.'

I can see Sollo's watching and thinking about only water as the ocean roars out there, so I say, 'You know what we said about God not being God really? It's in the bit where there's no separation?'

Sollo keeps staring at the sea, nodding slightly.

'Well we can do that ... '

Sollo sits staring at me and then lets out an almighty yell, staggers to his feet and raises his arms wide, with his chest all puffed out. 'Only bloody water! Yeah. Course we can do it. C'mon Nel!'

He reaches down and helps me up, and, holding hands, me and Sollo march back into the surf.

A sea mist hovers over the waves, and in the place where the sea usually meets the sky, it becomes blurred. Until it just seems to merge into one.

EPILOGUE

For those who would like background to the stories in this book, I offer the following notes:

Is this Home?

It is often difficult for aid workers who have just worked in refugee camps, war zones and poverty stricken countries to return home to Australia. Seeing our materialistic lifestyle with fresh eyes can be a trauma, for example walking down Woolworth's aisle of pet food. It's a shock that brings up a sense of alienation, and deep anger at our greed. My colleagues and I have found it important to support each other. One time, a bunch of us rented kayaks and paddled down the Glenelg River for a week of quiet, natural forest, gentle healing and listening to one another.

It's not just the culture shock that's traumatic, either. Often one's family and friends are not interested to hear one's story; they have no common background in which to place it. And, because the areas where one has worked are usually where people are oppressed, often there have been too many obstacles for the project's success. There are so many more constraints, such as widespread conflict and corruption, lack of infrastructure, extreme poverty, little food, and poor health. For many reasons, including the difficulties with working cross-culturally, success rates are much lower than similar work within the white Australian scene. For these reasons, returning aid workers are often exhausted, and their self-esteem bruised. It is vitally important that they have understanding and supportive friends to be able to debrief.

The character and name of my Dad's new wife were changed to protect her lovely memory.

MEXICO

PROJIMO was a project started in 1982 for poor village children with disabilities. Set in the mountain village, Ajoya, in Sinaloa, Mexico, it was the brainchild of David Werner, an American biologist, famous for his book *Where there is no Doctor* which was translated into fifty languages. David also wrote *Disabled Village Children* and it was this book that brought me to Mexico to learn about community-based rehabilitation (CBR).

In the 1980's the project was frontier stuff with its remote mountain location, the surrounding poppy farming, and the novel way David approached rehabilitation. It was hugely successful and run by disabled people themselves. With a goal of de-professionalisation, the project made sure that the one or two expatriate therapists who came there to learn at any one time were disempowered by being separately housed with non-English speaking families in their adobe houses. They were also actively discouraged from taking any leadership role.

Children with disabilities such as polio and cerebral palsy arrived on donkeys or mules from neighbouring mountain villages, and sometimes by bus from the city slums of Mazatlan and Culiacan. They were welcomed by the resident disabled adults. Working from their wheelchairs, these young people fashioned splints from plastic bus windows. They also made crutches, wooden walkers, seats, prostheses and wheelchairs for the new arrivals. They created opportunities for the children to attend school, mainly for the first time, and, in every way possible, they fostered self-esteem to empower these children.

I stayed in PROJIMO a few times during the mid 1980s, at one time taking part in a wheelchair construction workshop. Many of the young people became dear friends.

PROJIMO was the first CBR project of its kind in the world and its fame gradually spread, the concept replicating globally. There were many new ideas incorporated in its way of operating. One was to challenge the prevailing attitude that disability was divine punishment for a family's sin. Because the majority believed this, families often hid disabled youngsters out of shame. It was frowned upon for young disabled adults to have relationships with the opposite sex, let alone marry and have children. PROJIMO gradually turned this attitude around by supporting adults with a disability to run small income-generating enterprises in the village. They persuaded the village council to pave footpaths for wheelchair access; and the community built a playground that was accessible to disabled and non-disabled alike.

Gradually it became 'normal' to see people with disability out and about in the village and gradually male/female relationships were also accepted. One of the wheelchair-riders married and had a baby while I was there.

The setting of most of my Mexican stories are in Ajoya. Some stories are from memory, and only names have been changed, such as *PROJIMO*, *One out of Seven*, *The Chair*, and *Ishmael*. Others have composite characters from people I knew, or composite stories from real events. This was done to protect friends, but also to try and portray a wider view of the interface between the 'helped' and the 'helpers'.

The stories not in Ajoya are set in a project, Mas Validos[6]. This project was started in the slums of Culiacan by a bunch of young people with disability, university students, David and myself. The stories *One out*

6   In most of Mexico at that time, people with disability were known as Menos Validos, meaning less valued. Mas Validos, meaning more valued, was deliberately chosen to contradict such a demeaning label.

of Seven and *Angel* were taken from a diary I wrote in Culiacan at that time.

Mas Validos was an interesting project. The problem for people with disability in the city of Culiacan was a lack of government support, the prohibitive cost of any splinting, wheelchairs or rehabilitation and, maybe most importantly, the widespread stigma.

Although running the 'street clinics', as depicted in *One out of Seven*, was illegal, David facilitated them anyway, supported by the university students. In the space of that one 16-hour day, I watched David examine hundreds of men, women and children. The range of disabilities was immense; I had never seen many of the conditions before in my life. Poliomyelitis was still rife. We saw children with acquired brain injuries from encephalitis and meningitis. Large numbers of adults had bone and joint infections which malformed their bones over painful years. There were birth defects caused by widespread aerial spraying of tomato crops with dangerous pesticides, head injuries from accidents involving people crowded on the open trays of trucks, burns from poor electrical wiring, broken backs from falling buildings. In addition, there were diseases that were bizarre, such as 'frozen' sleeping sickness, elephantitis, and others that I had no name for.

David had brought with him medicines from USA and, because the project PROJIMO was a two-hour bus ride from the city, he was able to refer some people with spinal cord injury and those needing splints, wheelchairs and special seating to that project for extended stays. All these people were poor; all had had no access to help before this clinic.

The students also organised a wheelchair race down the main street of the city; they organised a bus trip to a playground in the city for children who had never been out of their homes. And they made sure television cameras recorded these events so that gradually attitudes could change. I accompanied a bus trip to the seaside and was humbled by the gratitude of those who had never seen the sea before, even though this was a seaside city.

It was these enterprises, David's enduring caring, and his popular writing that precipitated change for people with disabilities right across the world.

I am aware that unfortunately the situation in Sinaloa with the drug and gun running has become too dangerous for expatriates and others to continue with the project. As far as I am aware, it was relocated to nearby Coyotitan in 2000.

AJAHN SOBIN

The setting of the story *Going up? Going Down?* is Tequisquiapan, a village in the mountains, a few hours drive from Mexico City. My Thai teacher from the forest-monk tradition of Buddhism, Ajahn Namto Sobin, was running a meditation retreat as part of his quest to introduce Buddhism into Mexico. He was a very joyful human being and holds a special place in my heart.

These days, I do not believe in his lesson literally, but I do think as a metaphor it is a very interesting way to view life, particularly when contemplating the causes of prejudice.

I kept in touch with Ajahn over many years, occasionally visiting him in his home village in northeast Thailand after he returned from Mexico. One time I accompanied his entourage as he transported a big jade Buddha from Myanmar across Thailand from monastery to monastery. At the time he was organising a copy of the famous Bodhgaya pagoda to be built in his village. The building, now completed, has the jade Buddha at its centre.

In the story, *Unfinished,* my visit to his home village coincided with an annual ceremony. At that time the famous pagoda had not been completed. Its resplendent foundations looked ambitious in the little temple grounds.

INDIA

These stories come from Community Aid Abroad (Caa)[7] projects for the poorest of the poor in India from the 1980s to 2007.

In the 1980s Caa was a vibrant grass-roots organization. There was genuine partnership between local project leaders overseas and their Australian counterparts, always with an understanding that Australians took a back-seat role. In all projects there was a willingness to be innovative and there was a deep sense of trust.

In north-west India the rationale had slowly evolved from a Mahatma Gandhi model where a self elected 'guru', often a friend of Gandhi, would set up huge community development projects for indigenous Indians. It was the sheer numbers of tribal people who were mobilized that helped them to claim their basic civil rights.

Over the years this guru-led model changed to projects whereby local village people were trained to introduce new ideas into their own villages. These projects became multi-pronged, with micro-changes reinforcing each other. In this way, women were empowered to learn new ways of income generation and saving. Women and children were able to study at night when an hour of lighting was created from solar lights, methane gas collected from cow and human excrement, or mini hydroelectric schemes on mountain streams. Permaculture was adopted to grow food. Men gradually felt less need of alcohol to deal with the brutality of life, and all were learning about civil rights and ways in which these rights could be won within the legal Indian framework.

In this way millions of people found their dignity. They came to

---

7   Community Aid Abroad Australia merged with OXFAM Australia in 1995.

believe in their ability to not only survive but to cooperate and flourish.

My husband and I befriended Augustin Ullatil, the Caa project Officer for Eastern India at the time. Augustin helped us to understand the complexity and skill developed over many years in these projects for the most marginalized.

One such project, Nirid, was alluded to in my story, *Loving a Wife*, which I wrote from memory. It was a project initiated by four retired university professors from Bombay in an attempt to halt the need for mountain villagers in Maharashtra to leave their homes and become itinerant workers due to lack of food. The idea was to introduce forestry instead of the uncertain cash crops. Travelling once a week on two motorbikes to a handpicked village, the four set about planting saplings in one plot on the outskirts of the village. When the villagers' curiosity grew, they sat down with them and told of the future benefits of growing trees. For three years they chatted with anyone who came to visit and during this time not a single villager believed them—their precarious life went on as before.

The planted saplings matured quickly because of the monsoonal rains, and were soon to be harvested. When it became obvious that the amount of money received from the sale of one tree would be more than the profit from a whole field of crops, interest was finally sparked. Still only one farmer dared to try it on half his land, as it would mean a lowering of income for the initial years. When the others saw the change in this one farmer's life as a result of his experiment, the whole village converted. The village did well, and within two years, many hundreds of square miles were afforested around other villages. At this point, the introduction of clean water, sanitation, schooling and women's rights meant positive change was fast.

169

What the project demonstrated was that patience was the key. Of course people living below the poverty line are adverse to change, as it can mean literally a difference between life and death. Allowing the change to happen organically was essential so that trust could be built. Long-term funding was important, something the Australian government could well emulate when funding projects to support first nation people in Australia.

In the story, *Loving a Wife*, Patel was one of the four activists. He was eighty years old and still travelling back and forth to the project on the back of a motorbike.

The project, *Maisal*, was famous at the time we visited, and the story is taken from my diary. Some names have been changed in *An Exceptional Ordinariness* and I have only taken a wee bit of artists' license in *The Strange State of Babilu's Mind*.

SUDAN

There were, as far as I remember, 21,000 refugees from Tigray, Ethiopia, in the refugee camp, Shegareb, Sudan, in 1985. 7000 of them were under the management of Community Aid Abroad (Caa), supported by UNHCR and COR.

It was the time of Bob Geldof's Band Aid, which raised millions of pounds to support the 200,000 brave people who walked for four weeks from Tigray, with huge losses of life, in spite of the feeding centres along the way.

I think there is something about Australians, (although you'll probably say I'm biased). We tend to laugh when life gets tough. We laugh at ourselves and at others irreverently. It's not malicious laughter, nor is it lacking in compassion. I have yet to find a more caring and hard-working team than the one I witnessed working in Shegareb at that time, working to support the Tigrayan people to get on their feet again after the most horrendous drought and war.

Under the guidance of Helen Pitt, the work of the team was innovative and courageous. They set up tree nurseries to replant the desert when they left (the provision of coal for cooking from UNHCR was scanty and thus in order to eat, the people had had to cut down precious Sudanese trees). They set up a workshop to make sandals from rubber tyres. Traditional looms were introduced to the tuberculosis ward so the men could weave and the women could embroider in their traditional patterns, giving them something meaningful to do.

All major decisions about the running of the camp were made by the Tigrayans themselves, just as they had made democratic decisions in their own country. The Australians supported them and introduced some expertise and the medicines they lacked. Together, they set up the camp so that each community in Tigray could be replicated here with its own decision-making mechanisms.

It was not dictated to by Australia. It was true partnership.

The stories told to me by the nurses are as I remember them and I witnessed the first tooth to be pulled in the camp. (Names have been changed in the story to protect friends.)

Australia

In the mid 1980's I spent three months travelling through the Anangu Pitjantjatjara Yankunytjatjara (APY) lands in the north western desert country of South Australia. As an unpaid volunteer I was researching the need for physiotherapy services in the first nation communities. It was this experience that formed the basis of the fictional story, *In the Listening*.

Although I had taught myself Pitjantjatjara language and had completed a course on Aboriginal culture prior to my arrival, it was still an overwhelming culture shock. I now believe that no two cultures in the world are more disparate than white western and traditional first nation. For a privileged white Australian, it can be life-changing to re-think the meaning of identity and the word 'time', and to reconsider what constitutes 'family', 'house', 'ownership', 'illness causation' … and on and on. One gradually is led to see that every plant, animal, rock and human being is cared for and kept in balance by the mutual responsibility of cultural practices.

For me it was an immense privilege to be a visitor to a culture that carefully preserved this land for 60,000 years and I hope I've conveyed this deep respect in the true story, *The Teaching*.

The effect of cultural genocide caused by the white invasion and continuing white domination is poverty, cultural breakdown, overcrowded housing, poor health and lack of control. This leads to youth disillusionment. And in the 1980's this led to petrol-sniffing. Children as young as eight years old wandered around with cans of petrol hanging on string in front of their noses. Sometimes when they were high, the kids burnt piles of car tyres, or buildings during the night.

Sometimes there would be violence.

This was deeply worrying to the elders and the families. Ms Inyika, who finally persuaded the government to introduce unleaded petrol in 2006 (an intervention which finally put an end to the sniffing) said through a Pitjantjatjara interpreter, 'the petrol sniffing problem was like a monsoon rain that flowed down and affected everyone.'[8]

The story, *The Howling*, is as I remember it. I had only been in the APY lands for one week and petrol sniffing was rife. Trust was built as I slowly travelled through the lands; gradually I felt safer. It was a safety tinged with deep respect, which grew alongside my understanding.

Besides working in the APY Lands I also worked in other indigenous communities around Australia, doing research. Everywhere I went I could see the terrible cultural damage caused by white invasion. One of these was the catastrophe of separating old people from their land as they aged and died. Land is part of an aboriginal person's being. It cannot be separated without untold distress. Housing the elderly in hostels in the towns and cities and depriving them of their spiritual sustenance is cruel, although sometimes, because of dispossession, the only sad solution. The story *Calling Country* is a composite story, based on my observations in South Australia, Northern Territory and New South Wales.

---

8   Maddocks, Tom. Woman behind non-sniffable fuel rollout in Central Australia honoured 10 years on. ABC News. 26.10.2016.

CAMBODIA

It was David Werner who introduced me to Hans Husum back in the 1990's, when my Australian colleagues and I were writing a book to support community-based rehabilitation workers in war-torn countries. Hans, a Norwegian surgeon with a creative mind, had written a book to aid 'bare foot surgeons': that is, health workers with no more than six months training, who were doing emergency surgery in conflict areas. He also set up an innovative method to aid landmine victims. I was lucky to (briefly) be part of his team in northern Cambodia, my input being to introduce community-based rehabilitation into the mix.

At the time, the northwest corner of Cambodia had only recently evolved from a Kmer Rouge stronghold. It was a delicate time, when ex Kmer Rouge and Kmer were learning to live side by side again. My students were a mix from both sides, and with help from Hans, all were able to at last talk about their grief, fear and hope for the tenuous future.

The whole area of northwest Cambodia was carpeted with landmines at the time, especially the forested areas. Generally, Cambodian people were so poor that the government offer of 'free land' gave them no choice: it was either their families starved or they took a chance with the landmines when they attempted to clear the little plot offered to them. There were international landmine clearance teams in the area, often using dogs, but it was extremely slow, covering very small areas per day, not nearly enough to stem the tide of new farmers coming to clear land. The would-be farmers mostly set their newly acquired plot alight as fire was known to set off some of the mines, and in one day alone I heard four explosions near Pailin from the fires. Unfortunately, fire did not detonate all the mines.

To complicate matters even further, infrastructure was at a minimum; roads were atrocious, hardly passable even in a truck. There was virtually no industry to speak of besides agriculture. Access was too difficult and too dangerous for tourism, and tensions were high in the aftermath of such a bloody war.

At the time, more than 64,000 casualties of landmine and explosive remnants of war had been recorded in Cambodia since 1979. With over 25,000 amputees, Cambodia had the highest ratio per capita in the world.

It was into this environment that Hans came with his tiny Scandinavian team. They then set about training to create an innovative chain of survival for victims of landmines.

It worked well: victims' lives were being saved again and again where they would have died, and amputations were more rare and with less of the limb needing to be amputated. As part of the chain, they introduced income generating strategies, and in order to tackle the relationship between chronic pain and depression, early rehabilitation became a focus.

The whole interrelated program went from strength to strength. There were, however, obstacles to success due to many factors: corruption in high places, woeful infrastructure, extreme poverty, and criticism from the more high-tech Western rehabilitation centres in the faraway cities. However, on the whole, research showed it was highly successful.

For the story, *Burnout*, I used the setting of one of the district hospitals that I visited in 2010. The scene of the boy with an infected stump and lack of pain relief is true. Also true was the fact that at the time many patients were not getting enough food in order to heal properly. Otherwise, the story and all characters are fictitious. The wider story in the arena of aid is true enough, however. I had heard enough stories from the victims of landmines to be able to authenticate the wider picture.

I was also interested to explore the reasons for burnout in ex-pat aid workers. I saw this all too frequently in many countries. Burnout was not a factor in the actual project, as the project was run entirely by Cambodian people. Ex-pats in this case did not stay on the project (as I have depicted in my fictitious story) but would come, teach, and leave, in order that the Cambodians themselves could adapt their learning to their own culture and circumstances. In this way burnout and dependence was avoided.

As a result of the rehabilitation project in the district hospital at the time I visited, the Norwegian government guaranteed both adequate pain relief and nutritious food for all mine victims being treated in district hospitals along the Thai/Cambodian border. Hundreds of self-help groups for victims were being set up where members helped each other to find the courage to embrace life fully again. This particular project was one of hundreds that operated throughout Cambodia in support of mine victims.

THAILAND

In the late 1980's the Jesuit Refugee Service in Thailand was caring for refugees along the borders of both Burma and Cambodia. I stayed in their modest Bangkok centre and was humbled by their quiet and persistent dedication to improving the lives of all, particularly the young university students, led by Aung San Suu Kyi, who had fled the Burmese military junta crackdown, and those Cambodians injured by landmines when crossing the last 500 metres of minefield to reach the Thai-Cambodian border. I had already visited some of the Cambodian camps myself, one being the well-known Site 2, a camp of 145,000 people. This camp near the Cambodian border was surrounded by high, barbed-wire fencing and, although many international aid agencies were collaborating to provide the bare necessities, it seemed only to allow minimal self-determination. There was only one traditional healing centre that was run by the Cambodians themselves, with all the other scores of amenities and clinics run by expatriates. Thus, I sensed pervading helplessness, which, I was told, resulted in outbreaks of violence.

Listening to tales from the Jesuits, it seemed that they worked somewhat differently. They encouraged autonomy and as much freedom and self-determination as possible, particularly in the camps housing the young Burmese university students. Students were encouraged to use initiative, to grow their own food, and to move freely from the confines into the surrounding forest. It was deemed very important that they maintained their moral and physical strength.

The Old Jesuit, is as I remember it. I believe it must have been some of the camps on the Thai border of Cambodia the priest had visited.

No Man's Land

In a Royal Commission into aged care in Australia in the year 2020[9], it was found from the 10,518 interviews that 88% of residents of aged care homes were often lonely, 69% had no control over their lives and 40% got no visitors. It was also found that, of the elderly who still lived independently, 80% wished to remain in their own homes.[10]

'The large majority of older Australians consider themselves to be healthy, physically able to do what they like, and making choices to stay that way.'[11]

The two fictional stories in this section about ageing were written to help bring awareness to the joyful freedom that can come from self-determination.

---

9   Morgan, Roy. Exploring Human Behaviour from Every Angle. What Australians think of
    Aged Care. Royal Commission into Aged Care Quality and Safety. Research Paper 4.
    Perceptions of residential aged care facilities. July 2020. Page 27.
10 Where do Australians want to live if they need support or care? Page 47.
11 Experiences, expectations and preferences for older age. Page 33.

ACKNOWLEDGEMENTS

With all my heart I thank the people I met around the world who found themselves marginalized. They taught me about how to live with courage and kindness, and their example changed my life.

I'd also like the thank all who helped me create this book, with special thanks to my editor, Jane Robinson, for her extraordinary patience and skill, to Josefine Lea Dohm for the cover, Immortalise Assisted Publication Services for typesetting and proof reading, Ingram Sparks for publication, and to all my dear writer friends who have supported me for years as these stories emerged.

I'd also like to extend a warm thanks to my two teachers in the field: David Werner and Hans Husum.

Lastly I'd like to acknowledge the following:

Michael Leunig for use of his poem, *Another Way of Being*.

David Werner for use of illustrations from his book, *Nothing About us Without us*.

ABOUT THE AUTHOR

Liz Hobbs was born in Australia in 1941. She has always taken a keen interest in the lives of marginalized people, and as a consequence worked with village people around the world, both as an aid worker and as a physiotherapist. Her writing is grounded in Buddhist philosophy and her passion for the natural world.

Her publications include *Life after Injury*, 2002, *Falling into Sky*, 2019, *Almost Music*, 2023, and numerous short stories and poems in local anthologies.